MW00473507

Southern Literary Studies
Fred Hobson, Editor

Sewanee Writers on Writing

Sewanee Writers on Writing

EDITED BY Wyatt Prunty

)((LOUISIANA STATE UNIVERSITY PRESS
Baton Rouge   MM

Copyright © 2000 by Louisiana State University Press
All rights reserved
Manufactured in the United States of America
First printing
09 08 07 06 05 04 03 02 01 00
5 4 3 2 1

Designer: Barbara Neely Bourgoyne
Typeface: Minion
Printer and binder: Thomson-Shore, Inc.

Library of Congress Cataloging-in-Publication Data
Sewanee writers on writing / edited by Wyatt Prunty.
    p. cm. — (Southern literary studies)
Lectures originally presented at the first ten Sewanee Writers'
Conferences.
Includes index.
    ISBN 0-8071-2631-4 (alk. paper) — ISBN 0-8071-2652-7 (pbk.: alk.
paper)
    1. Authorship. I. Prunty, Wyatt. II. Series.
PN145 .S44 2000
808'.02—dc21

00-010080

The editor gratefully acknowledges the authors, editors, and publishers of the following books and periodicals, in which the essays noted previously appeared. A longer version of John Hollander's essay appeared as "Robert Frost and the Renewal of Birds" in *Reading in the Age of Theory,* ed. Bridget Geller Lyons (New Brunswick: Rutgers University Press, 1997). Donald Justice's essay was originally published in the *New Criterion* in 1997 and later appeared in his book *Oblivion* (Story Line Press, 1998). Wyatt Prunty's essay originally appeared in *Shenandoah* 46 (Fall 1996).

The essay by Russell Banks is reprinted by permission of Ellen Levine Literary Agency, Inc. Copyright © 1997 by Russell Banks. Anthony Hecht's "Paralipomena to *The Hidden Law*" is published with the author's permission, copyright © 2000 by Anthony Hecht. The essays by John Casey, Horton Foote, Ernest J. Gaines, and Marsha Norman are reprinted here with permission of the authors.

All photographs copyright © Miriam Berkley.

The paper in this book meets the guidelines for permanence and durability of the Committee on Production Guidelines for Book Longevity of the Council on Library Resources. ∞

Contents

Preface

Geographically, Sewanee occupies the southwest side of the Cumberland Plateau, overlooking rich farmland to the north and west and to the south and southeast the Sequatchie Valley, through which the Tennessee River meanders northeast-southwest between Knoxville and Birmingham. But for most people—certainly this was the case for Tennessee Williams— Sewanee is as much a name as it is a physical location. For Williams, it seems, since Sewanee was in a state that had his name and was bordered by a river with his name, Sewanee was locatable by word as much as map.

This is how writers have found their way to the Sewanee Writers' Conference—by the words they read and write and by word of mouth, all of which become magnified during a two-week stay in actual Sewanee. Gathered from the first ten conferences, the craft lectures collected here offer a range of perspectives on writing as practiced by various playwrights, poets, and fiction writers whose talents, like that of Tennessee Williams, have made the Sewanee Conference a watershed for developing writers.

Russell Banks discusses research in order to describe the constitutive power of the imagination. John Casey's wry treatment of simultaneity in art begins with Mozart, then visits Flaubert, Nabokov, and Chekhov in order to explain what Casey ends by calling the "dot-zap" effect. Ellen Douglas rehearses the way we "confront history every time we sit down to write a sentence" and the way the "shape" of history keeps changing.

Reviewing his long and distinguished years in the theater, Horton Foote recounts the many changes he has witnessed. Mr. Foote's perspective on the collaborative spirit of the theater enables us to understand why, as he says, playwrights "refuse to be defeated." Ernest Gaines explains why, broadly traveled as he is, his subject matter must remain the people of Louisiana. Anthony Hecht's wide-ranging response to W. H. Auden informs us about the ways both poets match talent with subject. John Hollander's discussion of Robert Frost unpacks the intricate subtleties of Frost's figurative thought.

Diane Johnson asks, "Write what?"—before she proceeds with wit and generous frankness to answer that question. Donald Justice reveals the way obscurity in "its simpler forms" can be the "presence of something hidden," which the reader senses and pursues. Romulus Linney describes the way craft and the unconscious are related and unfold through dramatic action. Alice McDermott uses Nabokov's *Bend Sinister* to demonstrate that "the heart at the center" of a piece of fiction is a vision unique to the writer which no rules overrule. Marsha Norman's witty list of dos and don'ts demonstrates the way a play's origin with the playwright and success with the audience live and die on the basis of character. Francine Prose explains the way that one right detail—appropriate yet eccentric enough to establish credibility in the reader's mind—earns authority for everything surrounding it. Writing about the figure of vacancy in the stories of Flannery O'Connor and Peter Taylor, I explore instances when what is not said becomes what is most said.

Sewanee Writers on Writing

On Research

Russell Banks

It's happened numerous times, but even so I'm still surprised after I've read in public from my novels, *Continental Drift, The Relation of My Imprisonment, The Sweet Hereafter,* or *Rule of the Bone,* when a member of the audience or sometimes someone from the press comes up later and asks me how I managed to do my research, how much had I actually done anyhow, and how much of the fiction was based on my own personal experience. Surprised, I suppose, because the folks who pose these questions are usually serious readers of serious fiction and poetry, are sophisticated and intellectual people, and thus one would expect them to understand that these questions are more usually and perhaps more realistically directed to scholars, historians, social scientists, and journalists than to fiction writers and poets. Actually, I wonder, are poets thought to do research? I'm reminded of a story told of the poet Robert Creeley, I believe it was, who, having read to a university audience a particularly long poem, long for him, describing the rise and fall of the narrator's marriage, was asked afterwards by a member of the audience, "Was that a real poem, Mr. Creeley, or did you just make it up?" So I guess, yes, in a sense poets too are thought to do research. But the point is, I do feel sometimes that I'm being asked, "Was *Continental Drift*, etc., a *real* story, Mr. Banks, or did you just make it up?"

I'm doubly surprised, although I probably shouldn't be, when I realize, on attempting to answer the questions and watching emerge on my questioner's face a look of utter puzzlement, that the questions regarding research are directed not to the middling-hip, ear-pierced, dirty-talking, contemporary American author of, for example, the historical allegory *The Relation of My Imprisonment* but to the middle-aged, bespectacled, bearded, befuddled professor who wrote *Rule of the Bone*. As if I would not have to go so far, then, would not have to do so much research to write a sentence like this, from *Relation of My Imprisonment*:

> But with regard to my theory about the paradoxical way in which my memory had come to function and not to function, almost as if it had come partially to withhold itself, because there was no one against whom I could test it with argument, except my wife, of course, who agreed fully with me on most things of a theoretical nature anyhow, I was not able to be sure that I was not merely constructing an elaborate disguise so as to hide some painful truth from myself . . . ,

as to write *this* sentence, from *Rule of the Bone*:

> There was other good stuff in there too—a twelve-pack of Bud kings, Fritos, some chips, and some Kotexes probably for the guy's wife which naturally caused Russ to make some of his cruder jokes but I didn't mind because for the moment at least we were like free, free to just be ourselves, driving fast with the windows down and the heater blasting, smoking cigarettes and eating junk food and drinking beer and cranking with Nirvana's "Serve the Servants" on WIZN.

Yet, to my mind, however much research (whatever *that* is—and my purpose here is to try to look at what it is, at least for a fiction writer) or however little I had done to write the novel *Rule of the Bone*, narrated by a homeless, fourteen-year-old, 1990s, drug-abusing wanderer from upstate New York in the ganja-growing backwaters of Jamaica, I had done just as much and as little to write the novel *The Relation of My Imprisonment*, narrated by the abstracted, moralistic, obsessive-compulsive coffin maker from the land of Plod on the Planet of the Puritans.

Well, surprise sometimes prompts reflection, and, reflecting on research in general while going back over my own particular backlist, as it were, those books whose process of composition I know best, trying to recall how, in creating that backlist of novels and stories, I myself engaged in research while writing them, so that for once, if only for myself, I might answer that apparently simple but deceptively deep and telling set of questions that come at one so frequently, usually after readings and in press interviews, but even from friends and students: how did you manage to do your research? how much did you do anyhow? and how much of the fiction was based on your own personal experience? They are serious questions, often put forward shyly and with other people listening impatiently for their turn, questions that, out of politeness, the constraints of time, and perhaps simply because we either don't know the answers or don't want to know them, writers tend to deflect rather than answer; or simply, we lie. Not I, of course; I'm by nature a deflector. But I feel guilty even for that.

Then there is this, and we writers are as subject to it as any mere reader, and it may invite in us a bit of shame or lead us to exaggerate somewhat the nature and degree of our research: something there is that loves a *fact*, admires a "real" poem instead of one made up, prefers the roman à clef to the conjuration, ranks the thinly disguised autobiography above the literary vision quest. It's an especially American hierarchy of value, I think—the predilection for "Just the facts, ma'am." Agents, editors, publicists, film producers, all of them, when a new novel manuscript starts to make its way slowly down the long, switchbacked, pocked, and pitted road toward the solitary reader, are secretly (and sometimes not so secretly) hoping against hope that the manuscript will turn out to be "Based on a True Story!" How much more eager we are, it sometimes seems, to see a fictional film, read a novel, story, or even a poem, when it's advertised or even rumored to be based on a true story. And if it can't be that, based on a true story, then we want it to be based on years of arduous research. We don't care where it's done, a university library is as good as the Himalayas. We probably don't *really* care if a novelist learned how to travel upriver into the heart of darkness from a book or by boat, so long as he did the research. Actually, that's not true: we prefer him to do his own fieldwork; we Americans do, and for us, after all, there's no substitute in our minds for eyewitness testimony. He's the real man, or woman, he was there. The Old Man taught himself Spanish and caught that fish himself, you know; learned to sail on Long Island Sound and went around the Horn from there, so call him Ishmael, give him the ears of the bull and the red badge of courage; read his fiction, folks, and weep. It's okay. Even if it's not based on a true story, it's based on fact and personal observation. He did his research in the field.

Well, the time has come to tell the real story, to spill the beans, at least my beans, and answer that simple set of questions honestly. In the last twenty-some years, I have published twelve books of fiction, set in places as far and different from Princeton, New Jersey, where I teach and live part of the year, as Haiti, Jamaica, South Florida, the decaying mill towns of upstate New York and northern New England, and even a place not unlike a seventeenth-century English midlands parish village; and now most recently I've written most of a thirteenth book of fiction, which is a historical novel set among antislavery agitators and abolitionists in mid-nineteenth-century America; and I have told stories about, and even from the point of view of, Edgar Allan Poe and Simón Bolívar, Haitian peasants, oil burner repairmen, part-time cops who dig wells and drive snow-plows for a living, Vietnam vets who run filling stations, middle-aged female bus drivers, paraplegic teenaged girls, Rastafarian drug dealers, and yes, coffin makers and mall rats.

And I have not done any research.

I'm not trying to sound Whitmanesque here, as if I contain in myself multitudes, or to suggest either that the curious circumstances of my childhood and a peripatetic early youth provided me with everything a fellow needs to know so that, later on as a sedentary adult fiction writer, he can write convincingly of Poe, Bolívar, small-town well drillers, teen-aged girls, Rastafarian drug dealers, and mall rats; nor that my father's work as a plumber took the family from New Hampshire, where I was raised, to South Florida, Haiti, Harpers Ferry, and mid-seventeenth-century England. Sadly, I was not so fortunate as to have had that disrupted a childhood or that interesting a life as a young man. No, what I'm trying to say is that when, after a public reading or during an interview, questions about research are put forward, they are actually questions based on what is generally known about how a journalist or scholar does research, and given that, my answer should be, "I'm sorry, but I don't do research."

It's not like "I don't do windows." I wish I *could* do research. I wish I could *allow* myself to do it. Which is to say, I wish it were somehow *necessary* to my fiction or could improve it, even a little. How I envy the scholar in her carrel in the bowels of Princeton's Firestone Library poring over musty, tattered texts, filling her three-by-five cards with lost lines, forgotten connections, obscure allusions, and unsuspected collusions, totally clear about her subject and what information she will need in order to master it, which will ultimately come, she knows, when she has read and annotated everything that has ever been written or said about the subject. And how I envy the anthropologist in the field, tramping through trackless jungles to encamp for months and even years with half a dozen naked extended families, living the neolithic life with them, learning their clicking, humming names for the beasts and plants that surround them, deciphering their choreographies and rites, transcribing their creation myths, mapping their cosmologies and observing the peculiarities of their mating rituals, wearing a loincloth, even, and body paint, and why not facial scarring, too? Not just the scholar and the social scientist—when it comes to the role research plays in their work, I envy the nonfiction writer and the journalist, too. Who wouldn't want to ride a train from London to Vladivostok for thirty days, or interview a serial killer, or hang with the camo'd gun-toting Freemen and militia pals of Timothy McVeigh, making interesting, shrewdly observant notations in a notebook, asking questions and tape-recording the answers, learning the actual truth, and cutting, shaping, planing, and honing it on a word processor back home into a five-thousand-word article faxed to the *New Yorker* or fifteen hundred words for the New York *Times* travel section? I've done it a little myself, some modest attempts at scholarship and at journalism, and loved doing it, and will no doubt do it again. But I have to confess, it's not at all what I do when I'm behaving like a fiction writer.

Let me try to recapitulate for you how in three specific cases I obtained certain information *not* given to me by the accidents of my birth, childhood, and young adulthood, information which has usually been thought to have come into my possession by means of "research." Let me describe how, but also more to the point, *why,* it came to me—that's very important—and what the information actually provided when it arrived—that's important too. In the novel *Continental Drift,* there is all that Haitian lore concerning *voudon* (or voodoo), all those details and descriptions of the Haitian characters' flight from Haiti's north coast up along the Caribbean archipelago to South Florida, and the scenes set in Miami's Little Haiti section; there is the Haitian creole that the characters sometimes speak to one another, paraphrased in English but left untranslated; there are the Haitian characters themselves, who obviously could not be less like me, especially the main Haitian character, Vanise Dorsinville, a young black third-world peasant woman.

In a later novel, *The Sweet Hereafter*, we hear the story of a number of parents in a small town in upstate New York who have lost their children in a terrible school bus accident, which, thank God, has *not* happened to me, a story told from four points of view: that of the school bus driver herself, who is a middle-aged woman; a Vietnam vet who runs the local service station and has lost his twin children in the accident; a teenaged girl injured in the accident who is now a paraplegic; and a litigator, a fast-track New York class-action litigator (some might call him an ambulance-chaser) who only coincidentally is in the process of losing his daughter to drugs.

And in *Rule of the Bone* we hear, in language as close to my protagonist's spoken speech as I could get it, the story of a year in the life of a homeless, abused, teenaged boy trying to survive in the malled-over world of mid-1990s America and who in order to do it has literally to leave America.

When I began *Continental Drift* in 1982, I was living in Concord, New Hampshire, not far from towns just like the fictional Crawford, New Hampshire, the decrepit, closed-in mill town where the novel begins, from which Bob Dubois, a white thirty-something oil burner repairman, packs up and flees for a better life in Florida. It's a town not unlike the one I was raised in, and Bob Dubois' situation and solution are not unlike those of my various male cousins and more than a few uncles. So I knew almost firsthand what it was like to be inside his skin and look out on the world; I knew what he would see out there in New Hampshire and what it would mean to him, and what it would not mean. And when he got to Florida, since I had wandered there in my late teens and not much later felt trapped by early marriage and fatherhood there, I knew, once he arrived, what Bob would see of the world in Florida, too, and what that would mean to him. The trouble is, back in Concord, New Hampshire, in my writing room, I was excitedly inventing a story that required a life and a world that converged with Bob's, the life of a Haitian peasant woman. (It never occurred to me to make her a Haitian *man*, even though I am a man: the form of my story and its themes wouldn't have permitted it; or a *Jamaican* woman, even though I had lived in Jamaica in the mid-1970s for two years, had made many Jamaican women friends, and at that time had never been to Haiti at all and knew no Haitians personally; it was the Haitian migration I needed, for reasons of language, religion, and history—for reasons of drama.)

Write about what you know, we're constantly told. But we must not *stop* there. *Start* with what you know, maybe, but use it to let you write about what you don't know. The best fiction writers seem to be great extrapolators; they start with a cue, a clue, an iceberg tip, and are able to extrapolate from the hero's entire soliloquy, the motive for the crime, the entire iceberg. How does Joyce Carol Oates, for instance, know so much about the sexual secrets of lusty, irresponsible, working-class white men? Or of African American, inner-city, male adolescents, for that matter? I mean, come *on!* Joyce is my good friend and colleague at Princeton; she's a shy, reticent, decorous person who, to the best of my knowledge, does not hang with the homeboys. She's *got* to be extrapolating all that information from some small bit of only marginally related information close to home, conjuring an entire world of quotidian data, speech, night moves, anxieties, desires, and hormonal aftereffects, drawing it out of what? A pair of men's undershorts flopping in the wind on a backyard laundry line, glimpsed by her from the train in Edison, New Jersey? I suspect so.

Well, I needed more than that for the Haitian half of my story. You will note, however, that my story in its bifurcated form and its twinned but opposite central characters and the controlling themes of immigration and the American Dream of perpetual self-renewal have preceded my need to know. They have in fact *created* it, not vice versa. It was strictly on a need-to-know basis, then, that I took notebook and tape recorder in hand and went into the Haitian bush, returned to the United States and buried myself for weeks in the Columbia and Princeton libraries, then flew to Miami and for several weeks wandered the streets and alleys of Little Haiti and rode fishing boats in Florida Bay. I even made a second trip into the Caribbean and island-hopped my way north from Haiti to the Turks and Caicos and Grand Bahama Isle, looking for locations, as it were. I worked like a film director with a script already written and actors already cast, looking to see what my Haitian characters would have seen and heard and smelled, and in that partial, limited way getting inside their skin.

We Americans usually associate that phrase, "need-to-know," with a politician's desire to protect himself from future investigations into "what did you know and when did you know it?" Nixon and Watergate, Reagan and Iran-Contra, and Clinton and Whitewater. As fiction writers our motives are different, naturally, but we probably should instruct our staff the same way Ronald Reagan instructed his (and Nixon should've instructed his): Don't tell me anything I don't need to know. As a fiction writer I have no need to master a subject, to become an expert on it, or to report or otherwise testify on it later; in fact, quite the opposite. Because if I had done enough research to master a subject, as would be required of a scholar of *voudon* or of Haitian migration to the United States in the mid-1980s or of vestigial cultural practices among second-generation Haitian-Americans in and around Miami, Florida, then it's very likely that my novel would have died a-borning. Its form and structure would have served no purpose but to organize data more or less coherently; its characters would have been case studies instead of complex, contradictory human beings; and its themes would have led me, not to the acquisition of a comprehensive vision of the larger world, but to a narrow, parochial didacticism or ideology.

E. L. Doctorow, asked by an interviewer how much research he did for his novels, answered, "Just enough."

In the case of *The Sweet Hereafter,* I started with an obsession created by a series of New York *Times* newspaper articles about the aftermath of a school bus accident in a Mexican-American community in south Texas. Here a great deal of research had already been done by the journalist: interviews with parents and other relatives of the lost children, lawyers, school and political officials, and psychiatrists, none of which, however, was of any use to me or fed my imagination in the slightest. It was the image of the lumbering, bright yellow school bus crowded with a community's unsuspecting children gone over the edge of the road and into a water-filled quarry—that's what obsessed me. The wrecked school bus with the lost children inside. A visual image. And it seemed to have huge implications and suggested meanings for me that had nothing to do with south Texas; it was, I thought, the opening scene in a parable about a village that lost its children, a chilling folktale that might describe and explain to me the nature and perhaps even suggest the causes of our culture's loss of its children, a loss not, of course, attributable to a school bus accident (although surely it has been accidental) but to something far more elusive and mysterious than that.

Early on, I determined that I would tell the story from the point of view of four different characters. There were many reasons, an important one being my desire to explore this event from the perspective of the community as a whole. (Two narrators would have polarized the story; three would have triangulated it; four implied many: it's a primitive counting system, 1-2-3-many, but it was sufficiently sophisticated for my purposes; five would have been redundant.) I decided to set my novel in a small Adirondack town, not unlike the town where I was then living six months a year and had come to know nearly as well as the New Hampshire town I'd used as a starting point in *Continental Drift* and some other books. (Write about what you know, I guess.) My four main characters in this parable of the lost children came to me rather quickly; it was a small town, after all, with a limited pool of candidates, and since each was to tell only a part of the story and in sequence, picking up where the previous narrator had left off, my essential form was set. Who better to begin the telling than the bus driver herself? And who better to follow her than a parent, who has lost not one but two children in the crash? And there had to be an outsider's perspective, so why not a lawyer in hot pursuit of a negligence suit? And then we need to hear, at last, from one of the survivors.

My themes, my main characters and locale, and my essential form were set; even my plot had been pretty well worked out: I knew I was aiming my story toward a resolution that I wanted, for better or worse, to decide the question of blame, legal and otherwise. Especially otherwise. What more did I need to know? Unlike some American novelists, Scott Turow, Winston Grooms, my friend John Casey, I have not been to law school and knew little of the legal language and procedures that were required by my plot and at least one of my narrators, so there was one important need-to-know driving me. But no other—or so I thought. I had at this time another friend than John who had been to law school, and who, while not a famous writer, was a fairly famous litigator, a specialist in negligence suits, a man who, as it happens, no longer takes on cases involving injury or death to children. Too painful, he says, even when you win. I told him of my need to know certain terms and procedures, and he provided me with a foot-high stack of old depositions that over the years he had taken from the grieving parents who had, through one horrendous means or another, lost a child or children in what was said to be an accident, an accident caused by negligence. I took the depositions home to my studio and began to read.

The legal language was there aplenty, and the forms and procedures as well. But so were the voices of the parents, as one after another they were drawn by the deposing attorney's questions to tell their terrible stories. I was frightened and profoundly moved by their stories; the details were enough to give a parent (and I am one) nightmares for a lifetime. But it was in reality not the stories themselves or the details that made me nearly weep with sadness and grow dizzy with fear for all the children I have ever loved; it was the way the stories were told, the language, the *style*. Each parent recounted his or her trauma in a flat, expressionless voice, devoid of self-pity, without any attempt to describe his or her pain or loss. Each parent narrated merely a careful, precise reenactment of the awful event—the mother describes closing the apartment door with one hand while holding the child's hand in the other, the left, she thinks, yes, definitely the left, because she's right-handed and always closes the door with her right, and the twenty steps to the sliding elevator door, where she lets go of the child's hand to press the button, and then the child leans against the elevator door and the door seems to swing in as if hinged at the top, its bottom apparently come off the rail somehow, and the child falling, and the door swinging closed again.

In seeking to meet one need-to-know, I had met another, one I'd not realized I even had. The pleasures of research. In these depositions I'd heard the true voices, the voices I needed to hear, the voices of parents trying to tell the very worst thing that any parent can imagine, something that I, although also a parent, could not have, would not have, imagined as fully without those voices. The constrictions and occasion of being deposed by an attorney had compelled these parents to tell the truth, the whole truth, and nothing but the truth, so help me, God, in the same way that, without realizing it, I had wanted my characters to speak; and so, as I wrote my novel, from the first word to the last, I imagined myself as an attorney deposing my four narrators, and in that way was able to speak as a novelist about something that to me as a parent was nearly un-utterable.

For *Rule of the Bone* you would think, looking at me, since I am now a graybeard, that I would have nowhere to start, if starting with what you know is what I was supposed to do. Not true. The child is father to the man, after all, so all I had to do was renew my connections to the child I once was, a turbulent, angry, confused fourteen-year-old boy, alienated by divorce, violence, alcoholism, and disabling neurosis from his family and any larger community, unprotected, uninstructed, and unloved, and take him to the place where, too frightened to go on, I myself had turned back and made the best of things at home for a little while longer. I think generally novelists suffer from arrested development anyhow, so it wasn't difficult for me to return to the nest of snakes that passed for my emotional state when I was sixteen and stole a car and ran off from my Massachusetts hometown for three months with my pal Dario Morelli, only to be turned over to the cops in Pasadena by the priest that Dario, a Catholic, had confessed to. And once there, once I was properly situated emotionally, certain aspects of my old 1950s teenaged language returned to my listening ear, aspects that are perennial in teen-speak—generally characterized by a defended, flattened tone that can shift meaning by adjusting, in microtonic degrees, from irony to praise, that can move inflection from one syllable to another and turn put-down into wonder, conveyed by means of a syntax that reflects suspicion and mistrust of the listener, withholding the important, self-revealing clause to the end of the sentence, sliding qualifier escape-hatches into nearly every adjective and adverb. The essential aspects of my narrator's voice weren't far from my own, once I started listening to it. Also, since I wanted my story to take my narrator, Chappie, a.k.a. Bone, gradually out of his family, then out of his town, and finally on to Jamaica, and perhaps complete the journey that I myself had only begun when I was sixteen and had thus been obliged to complete in other ways many years later—because of that, I knew that in the course of his journey he would be obliged to deal with themes of race and class. He could not travel to Jamaica and escape them. And I also knew the traditions I was tapping into, their forms and norms, their powers and limitations.

What I needed to give me full, easy access to Chappie's voice, then, to fill out the blanks in my knowledge of teen-speak, was mainly lexical: I needed to know the names of things that filled his world, his names for them. For, even though he was a white, lower-middle-class fourteen-year-old dropout from another one of those upstate New York mill towns, as I had been myself, it was now forty years later, and American society has been profoundly altered in the intervening years, so I made it my business to imitate an anthropologist of the mall, encamping there as much as possible and learning gradually my subjects' names for the many things that surrounded them—the herbs they use for medicinal, recreational, and religious purposes; their foods; their articles of clothing and adornment; even their weapons. I studied their native dances, read their master texts, diagramed their kinship patterns, and observed their sexual rituals. It was pretty interesting, man, as Bone would say.

What was surprising and in the end far more valuable to me, however, was that by having placed myself where I could see the world of family, community, school, even the larger culture that surrounds all Americans, having seen it from a kid's perspective, I was able to understand and clarify for myself the larger implications of my themes, especially the theme of America's lost children, who, as far as *they* are concerned, are not so much lost as abandoned.

Let me try to wrap this up more or less neatly by returning to my claim that I don't do research. I can't. I mustn't. Not in the way that people who don't write novels do research. For a novelist, research must always and exclusively serve the purposes of one's characters, one's narrative forms, story, theme, plot, and style. Not vice versa. From my point of view, scholars and journalists have got it all backward.

Of course, later, when the novel has been published, one is often thought an expert—on Haiti, or on *voudon,* say, or negligence suits, or mall rats and drug use—which has its occasional pleasures and perks, until you meet someone who really is an expert on these matters.

But then there is always the mystery of the thing you got right, when no scholar, no anthropologist, no journalist ever could have. There is the mystery, for instance, of how I knew that the captain of the boat that brought the Haitians across from Grand Bahama Isle, the man who tossed the Haitians into the water to drown a few hundred yards off the coast of North Miami, had a Jamaican mate who'd encouraged him to do this terrible thing—when the news clipping that inspired the novel made no mention of a mate, and years later there comes a letter from a Bahamian lawyer congratulating me on that particular detail and wondering how I did my research. How'd you know that? he wants to know. Because he was the very lawyer who defended that Jamaican and got him off and deported, and he'd had his record erased. And there's the pleasure of learning that the novel about the school bus accident is being taught in several law schools, strictly because of the accuracy of its portrayal of a negligence lawyer and the complex moral issues that he must deal with as a professional. They want to know if I'm one of those novelists who went to law school. And there's the pure delight of hearing a sixteen-year-old girl with a shaved head and nose rings telling me, "You got it right, dude. You got how it feels to be a kid. How'd you do your research anyhow?" she asks.

The only honest answer is, I don't *do* research. I write fiction. I tell stories. They are real stories, and I make them up.

Meanwhile Back
at the Ranch

John Casey

In general people who write prose fiction don't set themselves formal problems—at least there's not a list of acknowledged formal challenges like squaring the circle or finding the unified field theory. And there aren't even lots of neat forms, like fugues or sonnets or villanelles.

The only *definition* of a novel that I remember is an old joke: a novel is a long piece of prose that has something wrong with it.

There are *content* challenges. Lots of *content* challenges. Write about this region, about that class. The challenge I remember most clearly is that every so often some civic-minded readers wish that novelists would concern themselves with national life, with politics, with something bigger than intimate lives. But, in America at least, this challenge doesn't have many takers. *All the King's Men, The Last Hurrah,* and a few others. I don't think there's a really good novel set in Washington. *Democracy* by Henry Adams is too ill-tempered to be more than a satirical tirade, a shadow play of an essay. Maybe this lack comes about because novels depend on a character's free will and by the time a politician gets to Washington, free will is severely circumscribed. The choice part of free will is already spent, and what's left of will, however right and good, is just the effort.

There are some technical problems that fiction writers cope with—point-of-view shifts, first-person narrators and their blind spots—but these don't interest the general reader as much as they do the writer, and most of these problems aren't all that hard anyway, not compared to things like people, place, tone, or plot, which are big, even amorphous, but specific to each particular story.

However, from time to time one problem does pop up that may be the equivalent of a formal problem and may be, if not the Holy Grail, a neat challenge.

In the play *Amadeus* someone asks Mozart why he's so fond of opera. The answer is duets, trios, sextets. And what's so good about them? Mozart says, as I recall, that in a story or in a play only one person can speak at one time, but when people sing, the audience can hear and understand two, three, six voices at once—each voice with its own tune, its own emotion.

I was knocked out. I thought, gee, you sure can't do that on the printed page.

Later on I thought that you might get a little bit of simultaneity in a *play*. You can have one actor speak, and you can have another actor react.

"My dear," X says to Y, "I love you!" *While* Y looks terribly pained even as X speaks.

Y then says, "Oh, how sad!" and X's face is already a mask of grief. Y goes on to say, "For I must tell you that my heart is pledged to another!"

Meanwhile Z, lurking behind a bush, turns to the audience revealing a face so radiant with hope that Z doesn't even have to step on Y's line by uttering a single word, let alone the complete sentence "Oh joy! Could Y mean me?"

It's not Mozart; it's not Don Giovanni, Donna Elvira, Donna Anna, Don Ottavio, and Leperello all going at it together. But still I saw that a play could be more richly simultaneous than reading one word after another in a straight time line.

Then I remembered an effort from years ago. It was at the Iowa Writers' Workshop. A very smart fellow-apprentice brought into one workshop a story written in three different colors. Green—the thoughts of a man in a jealous frenzy. Black—the medieval bestiary he was reading at that very moment. Red—while at the same time the man's wife is rapturously embracing her lover. In the author's attempt to make all three colors happen at once, he had cut up each sentence into fragments so that you read a little green, a bit of black, some red and so forth. The effect of a single sentence was something like this:

"HE GROUND HIS / *unicorns and gryphons* / biting and kissing and biting / TEETH AND GRIPPED / *rampant on a field of azure* / her calves and the hollow behind her knee / WITH HIS RIGHT HAND THE GROOVED ARM-REST OF HIS CHAIR."

For a half page we were spellbound, or at least trying hard to be spellbound, but by the end of the page, everyone got a terrible headache. At least there was that simultaneity. Fifteen people with the same headache. Meanwhile, back at the ranch, everyone took two aspirin.

Some years later I read *Light Years* by James Salter, a novel that I loved, although a friend of mine summed it up as "luminously depressing." In any case I recognized an attempt at simultaneity, this time in more capable hands, a less raw experiment. In this short paragraph a wife on her way home from her lover's house:

> Her car was parked outside. It was afternoon, winter, the trees were bare. Her children were in class, writing in large letters, making silver and green maps of the states.
> Viri [her husband] came home in the darkness, headlights blazing his approach, illuminating the trees. . . .
> The door closed behind him. He came in from the evening air, cool and whitened, as if from the sea.
> "Hello, Viri," she said.
> A fire was burning. His children were laying out forks.

Wife. Car. Afternoon. Trees. Her children in school.
Husband. Car. Night. Trees. His children laying out forks.

We have the same quick shift of point of view as in the green, black, and red, and it is a *trio*, but it works better because there are two almost identical visual fields, with a few notes the same (car, trees, children) and a few notes different (afternoon/evening; their children writing large letters/their children laying out forks).

And of course our dramatic intelligence is appreciating the lies that bind.

It was after I read *Light Years* that I came back to *Madame Bovary* and found what is probably the most influential sample of this sort of back and forth near-simultaneity. It is in the scene of Rodolphe's first success with Madame Bovary, which takes place at the agricultural fair at Yonville.

The fair starts with Flaubert at his satirical best—a handful of Yonvillian characters puffing themselves up for the celebration, filled with the false sentiment and false consciousness that Flaubert despised—and loved to despise. The animal side of the fair, however, brings out an exuberance in Flaubert that makes him a master painter of large scenes. He gives us the whole fairground in tableau—the pigs, sheep, calves, cows, a magnificent bull, stallions, mares, foals. All the colors of the sky, the animals and the earth, and all the smells and sounds.

Flaubert is a wonderful knot: he loves the sensual and is in a rage at the misuse of the sensual.

The officials are farcical. There is a case of mistaken identity of the honored visitor, the one-gun salute goes off too soon, the *present arms!* of the guard sounds like a copper pot bouncing down the stairs, and the guest official begins an inflated speech.

The visiting subprefect says—and here you must imagine a pathetic man orating like Charles de Gaulle—"Messieurs: To the monarch, gentlemen, our sovereign, to that beloved king to whom no branch of public or private prosperity is a matter of indifference. . . ."

In the shadow inside the second-floor window, Rodolphe murmurs to Madame Bovary, "'[But happiness] comes one day . . . one day suddenly, when one is despairing of it. . . . It glitters, it flashes, yet one still doubts, one does not dare to believe in it, one is dazzled as if one came out of the darkness into light.' And as he ended Rodolphe suited the action to the work, he passed his hand over his face like a man seized with giddiness. Then he let his hand fall on Emma's. She withdrew her hand."

The orator's voice:

"For how should we clothe ourselves, how nourish ourselves without the farmer? . . . Who has not frequently reflected on all the momentous things that we extract from that modest animal, ornament of our barnyards, who furnishes us simultaneously with a down pillow for our heads, its succulent flesh for our table, and eggs. . . ."

. . . .

Rodolphe had drawn nearer to Emma and said to her in a low voice, speaking rapidly—

"Does not this conspiracy of the world revolt you? Is there a single *feeling* it doesn't condemn. . . . The purest sympathies are persecuted, slandered; and if at last two poor souls do meet, it's all organized so that they cannot join together. . . ."

Another orator goes on about primitive man eating acorns in the forest. Rodolphe gets to dreams, presentiments, animal magnetism. The orator to weaving, to the planted field, the vine. Rodolphe goes from animal magnetism to affinities. The orator does Cincinnatus at his plow, the Chinese emperor inaugurating the new year at the spring planting. Rodolphe explains that this irresistible attraction may be caused by their having known each other in past lives. He takes her hand. She does not take it away.

So we have two comic areas—political bullshit below and private bullshit above. Flaubert is successfully savage and disdainful in this duet of wrong notes.

But tucked into this counterpoint of bullshit—which by the way is having its effect on both Madame Bovary and on the crowd—tucked into a little niche there is a sweet internal song of Emma Bovary (who once daydreamed about a waltz partner, and then had a deep but unconsummated crush on young Leon:

> She saw in [Rodolphe's] eyes the small gold lines radiating from his black pupils—she even smelled the odor of his pomade with which he slicked his hair. Then a softness came over her—she remembered the viscount who had waltzed with her at Vaubyessard whose beard had given off this odor of vanilla and lemon, and mechanically she half closed her eyes to breathe it in. But in making this movement, as she leaned back in her chair, she saw in the distance on the horizon the old stagecoach "The Swallow" which was coming down the hill from Leux, trailing after it a long plume of dust. It was in this yellow carriage that Leon had so often come back to her, and by that very road over there that he had left forever. She thought she saw his face across the square at his window and then everything became confused. Clouds passed. It seemed to her that she was turning in the waltz under the flame of the chandeliers on the arm of the viscount, and that Leon was not far off, that he was coming, and yet all the while she was aware of the scent of Rodolphe's head by her side. The sweetness of this present sensation pierced her old desires, and they were blown, like grains of sand by a wind, into the subtle movement that was spreading over her soul.

Rodolphe completes his seduction after a few more days. He is heavy-handedly skillful and is quite pleased with himself at first. And then he becomes fearful of what he has aroused. That's an old—though usually interesting—story.

But it isn't Rodolphe as cad and master hypnotist who is the point of interest. It is Madame Bovary as self-hypnotist. And it is the *little* simultaneity of the viscount, the waltz, the chandeliers—and sweet young Leon, and the gold-flecked eyes and brilliantined hair of Rodolphe—it is that little inward spiral of accumulated imaginative desire—conveyed by sound, sight, *and* smell—that is the true centerpiece of the loud outdoor agricultural fair at Yonville with its broader counterpoints.

That little spiral has another simultaneity. The passage is an implicitly harsh judgment on Emma Bovary for her synthetic easy imagination, but Flaubert enters that imagination with a lot of sympathy. Along with her imperfect sense of things, Flaubert gives her vivid senses—and I don't think I'm imagining the undertone of his love for her, even as he sends her on her way from foolishness to foolishness to despair.

Another example of *how* prose writers attempt simultaneity, and then I'll say why. In this passage from *Speak, Memory*, Vladimir Nabokov gives a sketch of his father—a man who earlier was ultimately killed in exile by a right-wing émigré. This scene is also largely visual, and for most of it the tone is that of an amused, distant *raconteur*. But just near the end, Nabokov shifts the tone—in midair—to overlay his anecdote with something more passionate.

The old and the new, the liberal touch and the patriarchal one, fatal poverty and fatalistic wealth got fantastically interwoven in that strange first decade of our century. Several times during a summer it might happen that in the middle of luncheon, in the bright, many-windowed, walnut-paneled dining room on the first floor of our Vyra manor, Aleksey, the butler, with an unhappy expression on his face, would bend over and inform my father in a low voice (especially low if we had company) that a group of villagers wanted to see the *barin* outside. Briskly my father would remove his napkin from his lap and ask my mother to excuse him. One of the windows at the west end of the dining room gave upon a portion of the drive near the main entrance. One could see the top of the honeysuckle bushes opposite the porch. From that direction the courteous buzz of a peasant welcome would reach us as the invisible group greeted my invisible father. The ensuing parley, conducted in ordinary tones, would not be heard, as the windows underneath which it took place were closed to keep out the heat. It presumably had to do with a plea for his mediation in some local feud, or with some special subsidy, or with the permission to harvest some bit of our land or cut down a coveted clump of our trees. If, as usually happened, the request was at once granted, there would be again that buzz, and then, in token of gratitude, the good *barin* would be put through the national ordeal of being rocked and tossed up and securely caught by a score or so of strong arms.

In the dining room, my brother and I would be told to go on with our food. My mother, a tidbit between finger and thumb, would glance under the table to see if her nervous and gruff dachshund was there. *"Un jour ils vont le laisser tomber,"* would come from Mlle. Golay, a primly pessimistic old lady who had been my mother's governess and still dwelt with us (on awful terms with our own governesses). From my place at table I would suddenly see through one of the west windows a marvelous case of levitation. There, for an instant, the figure of my father in his wind-rippled white summer suit would be displayed, gloriously sprawling in midair, his limbs in a curiously casual attitude, his handsome, imperturbable features turned to the sky. Thrice, to the mighty heave-ho of his invisible tossers, he would fly up in this fashion, and the second time he would go higher than the first and then there he would be, on his last and loftiest flight, reclining, as if for good, against the cobalt blue of the summer noon like one of those paradisiac personages who comfortably soar, with such a wealth of folds in their garments, on the vaulted ceiling of a church while below, one by one, the wax tapers in mortal hands light up to make a swarm of minute flames in the mist of incense, and the priest chants of eternal repose, and funeral lilies conceal the face of whoever lies there, among the swimming lights, in the open coffin.

It's hard to find the exact point at which the seigniorial play turns into a requiem. Is it "and then there he would be, on his last and loftiest flight, reclining, as if for good, against the cobalt blue of the summer noon"?

Not yet, not completely—because we still get a bit of the raconteur in "like one of those paradisiac personages who comfortably soar, with such a wealth of folds in their garments...."

The sensual part of the reader's brain is still lit by "the cobalt blue of the summer noon" while the grammatical brain is alerting itself to the aptness of the simile: "like one of those paradisiac personages."

But the simile is extended and extended until it finally engulfs the anecdote: "while below, one by one, the wax tapers in mortal hands light up ... and the priest chants of eternal repose, and funeral lilies conceal the face of whoever lies there, among the swimming lights, in the open coffin."

The prose has a highly enameled texture, both the playful and the passionate parts, but the device itself is structurally neat and strong.

It is like a scarf joint.

If you want to join two pieces of wood—to make one piece of wood out of two that are the same size—you can't just put the butt ends against each other and toenail them together. They'll wobble apart. What you do is shave each end in a long gradual diagonal. Then you fit thin to thick and thick to thin, with glue and a few tiny flathead screws, sunk flush. And you have one piece, almost as good as if it grew by nature instead of by artful composition.

It seems simple, once you've learned, but it is a very ingenious, useful device and an elegant invention.

As Nabokov's two tones overlap, thick to thin, thin to thick, there is a duet—the thin part of his passion at first as faint as the sound of someone rubbing the rim of a wine glass with a wet finger, and then it sounds larger and larger, a somberness simultaneous with the cobalt blue of a summer noon.

But why attempt this simultaneity?

Either in *The Sirens of Titan* or in *Slaughterhouse Five*, Kurt Vonnegut describes books on the planet Tralfamadore, where civilization is better than on Earth. Each book is a dot. I can't remember whether you read it by putting it on your forehead near your third eye or on the tip of your tongue. I may be making up the tongue part, mixing up a microchip with a communion wafer. In any case, you stick the dot somewhere on you, and you get the whole story in one zap.

The ultimate dream in an Evelyn Wood speed-reading course.

Also the ultimate dream, I think, of a novelist. What Vonnegut was getting at is that a novelist's first notion of a novel is a dot—a zap that is not a concept, not a story; in fact it first exists without language.

During the long process of writing a novel the dot is always there, a star of wonder, westward leading, still proceeding, guiding the three kings over moor and mountain. And one of the things the novelist hopes for is that—after the reader is through the long process of reading—the reader is left with a dot-zap. The novelist might also hope for a reader with total recall of every scene, every figure of speech, every mot juste—but I think that's secondary to the dot-zap wish.

How would you like a lover to remember your love affair? How would you like to remember it? Total recall of every word, every gesture, arranged in chronological order? Or a dot-zap?

I may have gone too far; maybe the question isn't as rhetorical as I first thought. I suppose some might say it's both: all the moors and mountains all over again one by one *and* the star of wonder, the whole thing at once.

But the dot-zap *is* one of the effects we wish for; there is a deep urge to encapsulate a person, a year, a city, a novel, *not into an abstraction* but into a *chord* of simultaneous sensations. All that's on a large scale. And the dot-zap effect could be conceived by a novelist *before*—and achieved by a reader *after*—a completely linear narration. The foreshortening and overlapping needn't exist in the words on paper.

So there's still the question—why would a prose fiction writer want simultaneity in a short passage? It's not because simultaneity exists as the sort of acknowledged technical feat, as does, for example, the triple somersault for a trapeze artist.

There are reasons that arise from the nature of story writing. One of these reasons is that prose fiction has a surface texture that is often at odds with its ultimate goal. A story masquerades as sensible prose when poetic ecstasy is what it hopes for; it presents a visible world when its real goal is to conjure invisible forces; it pretends to be a chronicle, to subordinate itself to time, when its real goal is to create moments that are so compressed and crystallized that they arrest time, that they partake of God's time, in which everything happens at once.

So as a storywriter you're often doing two things at once, each of which is necessary but each of which would like to negate the other.

An example of this doubleness is physical action, a staple of storytelling. The problem with physical action is this: if a character is drowning, or having a tooth drilled, or making love, that character, under the stress of panic or pain or ecstasy, tends to become like *anyone*. Anyone at all, drowning, wincing, embracing. This is a problem because the point of a good story isn't just to create whiz-bang action with a crash dummy. The point is to use the action, the stress of action, to crack the shell of a character, of a character's factual life, so that the individual flavor of the psyche is released.

So willy-nilly, you're facing the problem of finding the details, the tone, the words that will sing both songs at once.

Sometimes the solution is displacement activity—a piece of action that seems legally, logically, even dramatically irrelevant.

Displacement activity is a term from natural history, subsection, animal behavior. The concept came from an observation of a male Siamese fighting fish. The observer knew that a Siamese fighting fish would attack and drive out of his territory any smaller fighting fish. He would, however, flee from another fighting fish bigger than he. The observer put a mirror in the tank. The fighting fish charged the reflection only to discover that it was exactly the same size as himself! He floated there in midwater for a bit, caught midway between his impulse to fight and his impulse to flee. Then this male fighting fish began, quite vigorously, to build a nest.

The observer was puzzled. The male fighting fish is indeed the nest builder of the family—is programmed to build a nest when stimulated by the female. But why now? The observer concluded that so much nervous tension had built up, both the nervous energy to fight and the energy to flee *and* the torque of wanting to do both at once, that the poor fish had to do *something,* so it short-circuited two of his instinctive responses and set off a third.

People do something like this, and fiction writers can use this behavioral tendency to write a scene that is apparently a sidebar to the story, but in which the writer can let us feel the pincers of a character's predicament.

In Chekhov's "The Lady with the Pet Dog," very near the end, the hero, Gurov, is on his way to meet his lover, Anna Sergeyevna. They are both otherwise married. Gurov was once a heartless rake, but now, in late middle age, he finds himself doomed to an adulterous, impossible, but deep and true love. Here is the sidebar scene:

> Once he was going to see her . . . on a winter morning (the messenger had come the evening before and not found him in). With him walked his daughter, whom he wanted to take to school: it was on the way. Snow was coming down in big wet flakes.
>
> "It's three degrees above [freezing], and yet it's snowing," Gurov was saying to his daughter. "But this temperature prevails only on the surface of the earth; in the upper layers of the atmosphere there is quite a different temperature."
>
> "And why doesn't it thunder in winter, papa?"
>
> He explained that too. He talked, thinking all the while that he was on his way to a rendez-vous and no living soul knew of it.

The story then goes into a lovely internal aria in Gurov's mind, and finally the agonizing sad-sweet lovers' meeting, as rich as the last duet in the opera of *Eugene Onegin.*

But it is the little father-daughter scene that I love most.

There's a neat, slick way of reading it: Aha. Two different temperature zones: a symbol of Gurov's double life. But Gurov could have noticed the snowflakes and temperature all by himself.

I like the several things made implicit by the daughter. She is old enough to understand what Gurov is explaining in his slightly stiff and pedantic way—an awkwardness that comes over this roué only when he feels deeply (otherwise he's an old smoothy). She is still young enough to listen patiently and affectionately to papa—she even asks for more: "And why doesn't it thunder in winter, papa?"

She is also what makes his love for Anna Sergeyevna so difficult. Gurov's wife has been presented as a social-climbing witch, a figure of satire; she is a legal-social impediment to his love, not an emotional one. Chekhov needed the daughter's voice to make a duet, to sing her own little theme and to evoke a notion of Gurov's other emotional allegiance, not as an argument or rebuke but as part of Gurov's whole life as it becomes for the first time rich with love and crisis simultaneously.

You might ask, whose displacement activity am I talking about here—Gurov's or Chekhov's? I think both; I'd guess that Chekhov was so immersed in acting the part that he felt Gurov's need to displace, and that Chekhov the dramatist had a sense of rhythm that gave him an awareness that the story needed to displace.

These various ways of including more than one line in a given fictional moment—whether by swift juxtaposition as in Salter's afternoon-evening passage in *Light Years,* or by a scarf joint of overlapping tones as in the Nabokov passage about his father, or by the introduction of displacement activity that releases two impulses by way of a third as in the Chekhov, or by any number of these techniques—all have something in common. I think it is an urge to charge a moment, to saturate it so intensely that it not only serves a dramatic purpose, but serves as an exemplar of how full a moment can be. It doesn't have to be sweet. Just confluent.

A friend of mine quoted to me the epigraph from *The Solid Mandala* by Patrick White. Patrick White got it from Paul Eluard. I don't know whether it is desperate or hopeful, but I think it has the essence of why writers attempt simultaneity: "There is another world, but it is in this one."

As for me: I, too, like all migrants, am a fantasist. I
build imaginary countries and try to impose them on
the ones that exist. I, too, face the problem of history:
what to retain, what to dump, how to hold on to what
memory insists on relinquishing, how to deal with
change.

—Salman Rushdie, *Shame*

Imaginary Countries

Ellen Douglas

Whether we are migrants like Rushdie or as fixed as pebbles in a piece of
pudding stone in some spot we think of as home, we confront history
every time we sit down to write a sentence, to make a new choice in a
story already begun or half finished, or to snatch at the glimmering notion of something brand new that nevertheless drags its own past behind
it. What to retain, what to dump, how to hold on to what memory insists
on relinquishing, how to deal with change. These are the problems we
face—sometimes consciously, sometimes weaving into our work over and
over again patterns that we may not perceive.

And history comes to us in such strange packages. If a writer is lucky,
she may run across another fantasist, a storyteller who shapes his own
history and gives it to her to put to use however she chooses. History re-
cedes from fantasist to fantasist like the infinite recession of images in
mirrors set opposite each other.

A long time ago an incident was recounted to me by an elderly black
friend who said it had happened when he was a young man during the
1930s, in the rural South, in the depths of the Great Depression. My black

friend, I should add, was so nearly white that he could easily have passed for a swarthy white man. Out hunting for food to put on his table, he had come across a family living in a tent in a clearing deep in the woods—a white man and his wife, a beautiful golden-haired woman ("Threads of gold," my friend said, "ropes of gold, falling all down her bosom, thick enough to keep her warm"), and their child. Here is the incident as I transformed and used it in *The Rock Cried Out*:

> To begin with, we stood around the fire and talked about hunting, and it was plain he'd been raised in the country. Then she pulled forward a box and invited me to sit down.
>
> "We haven't introduced ourselves," he said. "I'm Gene Hamm and this is my wife, Frances, and my little girl."
>
> "My name is Calhoun, Mr. Hamm," I said. Sometimes, if you call yourself by your first name only, it will locate you for the other person. But of course my first name is a last name.
>
> He pulled up a stool for himself. "Sit down, Mr. Calhoun," he said.
>
> "Calhoun is my first name," I said.
>
> "Calhoun what?" he said.
>
> So I said Levitt and sat. The little girl got her baby doll and a box made to look like a bed and sat down on the floor by him, and the wife began to fool around the fire, getting out a skillet and some meal and this and that. I tried not to look at her. What kind of white people are these? I said to myself, because I had never seen anyone like either one of them before.
>
> In a minute she asked me if I would eat supper with them and I said, "No, ma'am, I better get on my way shortly if I expect to kill a coon and get home before my wife begins to worry about me." I still didn't look at her.
>
> "You might as well eat," she said. "You can't hunt until dark."
>
> "You can look at her," he said to me. "You're not going to turn her to stone."
>
> "Sir?" I said.
>
> "My wife."
>
> I made my face as blank as I could. "Mr. Hamm," I said, "I'm colored. I don't look it, but I am." I could have added, "And even if I wasn't, I'm a young man and she's a beautiful woman."
>
> "I know," he said. "I knew you must be colored as soon as you spoke outside about the white people who own the land."
>
> These are crazy people, I thought, and I've got a family to raise. I better get out of here. I continued to look at the floor and began to gather my feet under me to get up.
>
> "Hasn't she got the most beautiful hair you ever saw?" he said.

I didn't raise my eyes. "Yes, sir."

She had her back to us, cooking something on a little Coleman stove that was sitting on the bricks next to the fire. She spoke out in a low voice—the softest sweetest voice I had almost ever heard. "Don't pay any attention to him," she said. "He's just trying to be friendly."

"Come over here, darlin," he says to her and she comes over to where we're sitting and he pulls her down between us, picks up a strand of her hair, and passes it through his fingers. "You want to touch it?" he says.

"Mister," I said. "I wouldn't touch her hair unless you picked my hand up and laid it on her head."

"Do you mind, Frances?" he said.

And she said, "Of course not."

And he did. Picked up my hand and laid it on her head.

I felt like my hand was on fire. I held it there on her head a minute, looking at him, not her, and then drew it back.

She got up and went back to the stove and in a few minutes she brought plates for all of us. The little girl put her baby doll to bed and we all sat there around the fire and ate supper.

While we ate, he began to talk to me as openly, as trusting, as if he'd known me all his life.

This incident (true—or told to me as true by a storyteller famed in his neighborhood for his narrative skills) was told to me years after it happened and years before I used it. It stuck persistently in my mind: the image of the white woman with the beautiful hair, of the sealing of a bond of common humanity among three people in that dark place and time by laying the black man's hand on the white woman's head. I knew I would someday put it to use.

Time passed. Other stories and scraps of history came my way.

In the late sixties I was present when one of my sons was accosted outside a country grocery store in south Mississippi by a drunken black man who was so sure of his status in that threatening world that he could call a white boy to account for his appearance. "You look like a girl," he said, "with that long hair and pretty face and all. A girl or a gobbler." This too went into my memory.

Shortly afterward I began meditating on a possible new novel. I had just finished *Apostles of Light*, a novel set in an old people's home, and I wanted to write about young people for a change. I was concerned obsessively then with the world my husband and my sons and I were living in, the history we were living through: with the Vietnam War, the civil rights movement, all the tragic complexities of our time. I didn't have a story, a set of real or imaginary events. I had my knowledge of a particular part of southwest Mississippi where the two incidents I have just described occurred. I had other tales, true and untrue, of that world and the people who lived there. And I had my sons who grew up in the sixties and early seventies, and their cousins and friends and girlfriends, whose lives I was witness to. I suppose I might say, hesitantly, that the place itself—Natchez and Adams County, Mississippi—was my imaginative home. I had grown up living elsewhere, but visiting my grandparents in Natchez—summertime visits to a world curiously itself that use and familiarity had not rendered commonplace.

Imaginative home or not, why did I decide to put my story about young people coming of age in the sixties and early seventies in that place? Natchez, I knew, was a dangerous spot to claim. It meant burdening myself with clichés—moonlight and magnolias and hoop skirts and aristocrats and mint juleps—the very essence of maudlin romance. But we try for detachment—building imaginary countries and imposing them (the very act implies detachment) on the ones that exist, even those that exist as products of someone else's corrupt imaginings. I recall my mother's ironic assessment of her girlhood home. "What you need to break into Natchez society, to become one of us," she often said, "is a white linen suit and a bottle of whiskey."

And besides, in the late twentieth century even if we stay in the homes of our parents and grandparents, even if we have taken in their myths and their history with our mothers' milk, we are all migrants. However known, however familiar our places may be, we see them transformed again and again at a dizzying rate, and again and again we must find ways to "deal with change"—with wrenching change. Natchez, for example, has been transformed a couple of times in the past decades, first by a lucrative oil strike that made millionaires of some of her land-poor "aristocrats," and then by the collapse of the oil patch, which impoverished them again. Lately, since restrictions on riverboat gambling have been relaxed, Natchez bids fair to become a gamblers' paradise, a Las Vegas of the Mississippi, as if her nineteenth-century frontier life were being reenacted in Disneyland.

For my novel, the very existence of the cliché, the romantic myth, would be useful. The one-time cotton plantation where my father lived as a boy now had on it not only woods and pastures, abandoned cotton fields, and a pre–Civil War house, but also a federal soil-conservation lake, several pumping oil wells, a tree farm, and some scrawny cattle. It would eventually have on it a space surveillance station made up by me.

These are all possibilities for building imaginary countries and imposing them on mythical countries, which can be imposed in turn on what purports to be a real country: that haunting, lovely, rural Deep South country of cedar and poplar and pine and magnolia trees, of wood fern and yellow jasmine and trillium and dogwood and maypops; of chinaberry trees—a haze of fragrant lavender in the spring; of skunks and foxes and now, armadillos and coyotes and fire ants (new migrants from Texas and Mexico). It is a world familiar and dear to me, but vanishing and reforming itself every day. What's there and how can I use it? Will anything stay still?

Well, there is the old house. And there is the history of the place where the house stands, and its occupants—owners and slaves, farmers and tenants, back to the Spanish grant in the late eighteenth century. But is it history? Possibly. Myth? Certainly. Lies? No doubt.

And there are my sons who did, in fact, have a romantic relationship with that place, each of them living alone at one time or another in a cabin they put together out of abandoned tenant houses. In the surrounding county there are the kind of people, black and white, who have lived there for two centuries, their relationships to one another changing, changing: cotton farming giving way to cattle, cattle to oil, oil to tree farming; black churches that were burned in the summer of 1964 and white churches that were home to the Klan. No story yet, but what a rich vein to mine.

What happens to all this material in the process of writing a story or a novel—building an imaginary country? Every writer has (as it should perhaps go without saying) a stance—moral, ethical, political, emotional, artistic—arising from a lifetime's experience and reading and thought, and from the practice of one's craft. The stance may—must—change again and again, but at any given moment it is always at the heart of the fiction. And then there are the insights, the convictions that inform this project, insights that in part one begins with and in part result from the exploration of the material—the act of writing the book. So one sets in train a long meditation. How to begin? And then, what next?

In this case *next* turned out to be another scrap of memory—the memory of talking with an old black man who plotted his stories by giving them echoes of, making them conform to, sacred myths. The events in his own life and the lives of his extended family, as he told of them, were often shaped by his knowledge of tales from the Bible. My friend was like the narrator of the story of Jacob going in search of a bride and repeating in part the journey of his father, Isaac. He sometimes shaped his tales by repetition. He knew that the most deeply significant tales from the past were reenacted in every generation. Sarah and Abraham's late-born son became one with his own late-born son. And I, guided by his techniques, began to think of using myth in this way, began to think of how I would use the character Noah in my novel. He would be a teller of tales, would transform history to make it conform with sacred myth and thus become a story.

From the beginning I was sure that the place and time would furnish me, as I meditated, with a kind of unity. Only certain kinds of things could happen here, only certain kinds of people lived here. I was sure, too, that place and time would give me images and controlling metaphors. But stories? I'd have to come up with a novel-sized story or stories, and with a plot—a plan for arranging my stories to make their meaning clear and to make a pleasing and seamless whole.

I began to take notes on characters and to jot down possibilities, to think about the ways they might be involved with one another. For me this process, discovering one's book, is months long, sometimes a year-long undertaking. And it is very often a process of combining. For example, one of the first acts that seemed inevitable to me in *The Rock Cried Out* was the combining of the characters in the two incidents I've recounted above. The arrogant fellow who accosts the white hippie and the man who discovers the mysterious white couple in the woods should be the same man. But what would his life story be? That, of course, pointed me in the direction of a story. And the white hippie? Who was he? Not my eldest son, who was, in fact, not a hippie, but a recently discharged officer in the United States Army, back from Thailand and dressing at last, after three long years in the service, precisely as he wished. Again, I combined—the faces and voices of young people I knew—to shape my hero. As it turned out, he had the face and hair of a beautiful nineteen-year-old lad who had voluntarily, foolishly, gone off into the Marines in 1967, and the circumstances of a young conscientious objector friend of one of my sons who had served his time in the insane asylum at Whitfield, Mississippi. He had my youngest son's big feet, planted firmly on the ground. And, most important, his voice.

To me it has always been useful to have, sounding in my ear so to speak, a voice that is appropriate to my fictional character. In this case, although the incidents that I began to dream up were for the most part not incidents that had occurred in my son's life, the voice is his, as I heard it, as it lives in my memory. Against his voice I could test my fictional hero. Is the vocabulary consistent? Are the speech rhythms right? Are the metaphors, the slang, the small ironies, the particular kind of humor, consistent with the voice echoing in my ear, in my head? Nothing, it seems to me, has been more useful in realizing a convincing character than the constant sound of a voice against which to test him or her. The voice is the glue that holds the character together.

But voice doesn't invent story or construct plot. Voice gives one only the language and tone of a particular character. And it's on story and plot that I most often feel myself foundering. And story and plot, whether or not I'm good at inventing them, I am committed to. I want, above all, to tell a true story and to tell it well, to invent the true lie that is at the heart of every good fiction.

Here, too, memory, whether it holds onto or distorts or insists upon relinquishing, serves me in good stead. Memory has taught me how to write fiction. I knew this, as I think every writer of fiction knows it, from the beginning, instinctively, without articulating it. Memory has everything to do with the shaping of a story, with its form.

Suzanne Langer seems to me the thinker nearest the mark regarding how we make fiction and why we make it as we do. She speaks of literature as being in the mode of memory and of fiction as being the art that gives form to experience, to lived life, as music gives form to sound and pulse in time, and as dance uses music and bodies to organize space in time. Reading, we live the experience of the book, and afterward it lives in our memories. And for the writer, the form of a story is governed by the forms memory uses.

Memory calls up scenes and images, dramatizes, connects scenes and images to bodily sensations. Memory organizes our past just as plot organizes our fiction. Memory teases out significance, abandons the irrelevant, summarizes, suppresses, distorts, invents. Memory is the imaginative creation and recreation of the individual's experience of the world. It plots our lives. And chronology is as irrelevant to memory as it is to plot. We range over our past not in an orderly sequence of days, but associatively. A word, an odor, an uneven stone stepped on in a courtyard calls up a whole world. Just so, the writer ranges over her material.

Association, connection, combining are the keys to my method, the keys to finding the significance and shaping the stories that drift into my ken, whether from observing a scene in a country grocery store, or hearing a tale of a mysterious couple living in a tent in a swamp, or reading of a murder in yesterday's newspaper. Or—and this *or* opens a treasure trove—my memory of all I've read: history, myth, fairy tale, novel, poem. For these memories, too, shape the work. So, from the mine of memory I dig every image, every sound, every sensation, every feeling, every odor, every event, every word, every sentence, every paragraph. The ore passes through the meditative process of sorting and screening, rearranging, distorting, inventing, and I always hope, refining, purifying. I want a ringing sterling metal for the finished product.

Of course, like any rememberer (unless she's a saint), I am dishonest. I'm tempted to punish characters I dislike—especially if they are based, however tenuously, on real people whom I also dislike. I'm tempted, above all, to be comfortable, to write what will not disturb me. And to make myself, the novelist, the heroine of every story, to direct the reader to think of me, not only as a brilliant and perceptive writer, but as a noble (not to mention beautiful) human being.

Ah, but it doesn't work. Readers are too clever. They would catch me out.

And besides, I always come back to the struggle. To make a fiction, yes, but a true fiction. To create a form that bears witness in every part and in its seamless whole to whatever truth I can find at the center of my world, to a truth that makes us say: Yes, that's how things are. I'd never thought of it before in exactly this way, but that's how things are.

My hero, Alan, and Noah, talking together in the last chapter of *The Rock Cried Out*, put it like this. Alan is speaking:

> [I]t's early April now. The dogwood trees are in full bloom; the green light that glows in those pure white petals must be the kind of light that shines in the eyes of God. The yellow jasmine vines and redbud trees flicker with the fire of spring. And down in the bottoms of the deep ravines the swamp maples are flaming, the oak trees tasseling gold. The woods are burning with life.
>
> I went (as I always do when I come back to the cabin) to see Noah yesterday. I think it's more important every year to go to see Noah, to talk with him. He'll be gone—soon. I want to hear everything he has to say before he dies. And he wants to tell me all he knows. Yes, he wants to tell me, so that I will *remember*. He tells me most things over and over to impress them on me, because he is the onliest one left, the onliest one who can tell me....

He had a heart attack last year and while he was in the hospital, he had a vision.

"Twas like they didn't know I was alive," he said. "Standing around talking about me and moving me here and yawnder. Seemed like they put me in a box and hook these wires to my ears, sent a shock, like lightning, all through me, and I hear a Voice say, 'Noah. Noah.' And I say, 'Lord, here am I, a *old* man. Ain't it late in the day for You to be speaking to me?'

"But He says, 'Noah, child, I ain't letting one word of yours fall to the ground, and that's my promise to you. And I want you to tell that boy of yourn, Alan, all you know. . . .'"

He gave me a sly look.

"Noah!"

"I ain't even hardly *started* telling you all I know," he said.

He was out of the hospital and home in two weeks, plowing his corn in two months.

My papers now are spread around me in neat stacks, and I am adding a sentence here, a paragraph there, trying to put in everything, to ask and answer as many questions as I can. I can't help feeling the urge of the storyteller to tie up loose ends, to write, "And everybody lived happily (or unhappily) ever after." Plus the urge of the moralist to make a point, of both to give the tale a shape.

But the shape is still changing. Only the finished—the dead—have a finished shape. Not even the dead, crumbling to earth. As Noah says, "The earth is strong, boys."

Next year the dead will be flaming in the April trees.

How To and How Not To: Some Lessons Learned Along the Way

Horton Foote

When I began writing plays, the Broadway playhouses were full nine months of the year. (There was little air conditioning then, so most plays weren't expected to survive the New York summer heat.) There were plays by Maxwell Anderson, Robert Sherwood, Elmer Rice, Sidney Kingsley, S. N. Behrman, Clifford Odets, and Franz Werfel and occasional revivals of Shakespeare and Ibsen. One notable production was Alla Nazimova's *Ghosts*, followed by her not-so-effective *Hedda Gabler*. Eva le Galliene's Civic Repertory Theatre had closed because of the Depression a few years earlier, and repertory productions of Chekhov, Ibsen, and other European playwrights were rarely to be attempted again.

It was le Galliene's productions of Ibsen's *Hedda Gabler*, *The Master Builder*, and *A Doll's House* that I had seen earlier in California, when I was at the Pasadena Playhouse studying acting, that first gave me a sense of the power of theater.

Up until then, like most young actors, I was interested in a play only if there was a good part for me. In these three Ibsen plays there was nothing for a seventeen-year-old, and for the first time I realized a play existed for something more than to satisfy an actor's ego. After all these years, the power of those Ibsen plays is still vividly with me.

In New York a year or so later, I began studying acting with three Russians: Tamara Daykarhonova, Vera Soloviova, and Andrius Jilinsky, and although I was unaware of it at the time, here began my first lessons in playwriting. These teachers, all trained by Stanislavsky, taught me as an actor to respect the playwright and to search each play for its through line, its beats and actions.

A group of us from Daykarhonova's studio formed an acting group called the American Actors Company. Mary Hunter Wolfe was our director, and we chose to do plays by American playwrights: Paul Green, Lynn Riggs, E. P. Conkle, and Thornton Wilder, all of whom were rarely produced by the commercial theater. The members of the company were from all parts of America, and we attempted through a series of improvisations to show each other something of the particular sections we came from. I was from Texas and I did a number of improvisations about life there. Agnes De Mille came down to do a production with us and saw some of my improvisations and suggested that I should try using some of the material in a play. I wrote a one-act play with the lead for myself and the company produced it. Robert Coleman of the New York *Mirror* came to see it and praised the play and my performance. Here I learned my first lesson of what not to do: for I had taken a literal situation, called it *Wharton Dance* (Wharton being the name of my hometown), and used the real names of people. My mother, pleased with the attention of Mr. Coleman, asked for a copy of the play. I sent it to her and she eagerly shared it with her friends, some of whose children were characters in the play, and they were not pleased. So I learned early on—never use real names, be cautious of using a real place, and never be only a reporter in telling your story. That summer I went back to Texas and wrote a full-length play called *Texas Town*. This time I gave my town another name, carefully avoided naming any characters after anyone I knew, and the plot of my play, though based on what I'd seen and observed, was not so literal; it was more than reporting. That fall the company produced the play and this time Brooks Atkinson, the critic of the New York *Times* came to see the play and praised it. The company wanted me to give up acting and devote my time to writing. This was the time of the Carolina Playmakers and other such regional groups, who had a theory that everyone had at least one play to write—the folksier the better. I had a horror of being a regional playwright, and I was afraid I might prove all too true the Carolina Playmakers' theory of one person, one play.

I had written from instinct and had no technical skills whatsoever. Lynn Riggs was a friend of mine whom I went to for advice, and he said, "Just trust your talent and write about what you know." A little later I met Tennessee Williams, who was just getting recognized, and when I asked him for advice on how to write, he laughed that hysterical laugh of his and never answered the question. Later he said, "Everybody has to find out for themselves." He said his agent, Audrey Wood, had insisted he take a course at the New School with Theresa Helburn and Lawrence Langner of the Theatre Guild, and it was a waste of time. He said, "Find writers you admire and study them." Some of the writers he was studying were Chekhov, Hart Crane, and D. H. Lawrence.

Fortunately, my training as an actor had given me a sense of play structure. The playwrights I admired, Strindberg, Ibsen, and Chekhov, were each vastly different. What were these differences? How did they achieve them? I sensed it was beyond structure. It was something innately unique in each of them. When I asked Mary Hunter Wolfe about this, a very learned and articulate lady, she said each had developed his own thematic interest and his own style. I began to ask too many people too many things, and I got back a barrage of *how to*s. How to grab an audience. How to have a hit. The *how to*s were endless.

And the *how to*s in New York City in 1936 had little interest in Hart Crane or D. H. Lawrence. Ibsen was depressing to them, and besides, in spite of Nazimova's success in *Ghosts*, Ibsen, they told you over and over again, never made a dime. Chekhov couldn't be made commercially successful either, even with a star, and as for Strindberg: "My God! Commercial suicide."

Among the more successful playwrights then were Maxwell Anderson, S. N. Behrman, Elmer Rice, Lindsay and Crouse, Robert Sherwood, Sidney Kingsley, Rachel Crothers, and Lillian Hellman. Clifford Odets had a special niche. He was known as a radical and an innovator, loyal to the Group Theatre and its way of working. Harold Clurman had this to say about Odets:

> Clifford Odets has not only an energy that is characteristically of our age, but he is of a generation that has come to look critically and participate

actively in the day-to-day struggles of our cultural and social world. His most important contacts in the past five years have been with artists and craftsmen, all in search of a way of life which would permit them not merely to "exist" (that is, "to do as the Romans do"), but to give free range to their sensibility and intelligence in organizations that might bring some sort of constructive order into the chaos of our artistic and social life.

Odets was a child of the Depression, and his characters in his early plays were rooted in the Depression and its problems. This is an example of his dialogue from his play *Awake and Sing,* a scene between Bessie Berger and her son Ralph:

> *Bessie:* So go out and change the world if you don't like it.
> *Ralph:* I will! And why? 'Cause life's different in my head. Gimme the earth in two hands. I'm strong. There . . . hear him? The air mail off to Boston. Day or night, he flies away, a job to do. That's us and it's no time to die. [*The airplane sound fades off as* MYRON *gives alarm clock to* BESSIE, *which she begins to wind.*]
> *Bessie:* "Mom, what does she know? She's old-fashioned!" But I'll tell you a big secret: My whole life I wanted to go away too, but with children a woman stays home. A fire burned in *my* heart too, but now it's too late. I'm no spring chicken. The clock goes and Bessie goes. Only my machinery can't be fixed.

Most of the other playwrights, too, were political liberals of varying degrees. Many of them tried to use the social causes that interested them as themes for their plays, sometimes succeeding, more often not. Lillian Hellman did succeed with her plays *The Little Foxes* and *Watch on the Rhine*, the latter about an anti-Nazi refugee, Kurt Müller, who has decided to leave his wife and children in America and go back to Germany and fight Nazism. He gives this speech to his children at the end of the play:

> *Kurt:* [*Shakes his head.*] Now let us get straight together. The four of us. Do you remember when we read *Les Misérables?* Do you remember that we talked about it afterward? . . . Well. He stole bread. The world is out of shape we said, when there are hungry men. And until it gets in shape, men will steal and lie and—[*slowly*] and—kill. But for whatever reason it is done, and whoever does it—you understand me—it is all bad. I want you to remember that. Whoever does it, it is bad. [*Then gaily.*] But perhaps you will live to see the day when it will not have to be. All over the world there are men who are fighting for that day. [*He picks* BODO *up, rises.*] Think of that. It will make you happy. In

every town and every village and every mud hut in the world, there is a man who might fight to make a good world.

You can find a variation of these hopeful summing-up speeches in other plays of that time: Sidney Kingsley's *Men in White,* Elmer Rice's *Judgment Day,* Gow and d'Usseau's *Tomorrow the World.* Here is Maxwell Anderson's variation in *The Eve of St. Mark:* "Allright boys. You go and make things over your way. We old folks, we'll stay here and milk the cows and run the bales. . . . Make a new world, boys! God knows we need it!"

These playwrights came from various backgrounds—reporters, lawyers; Ms. Hellman had been a play reader for the producer Herman Shumlin; Sherwood had worked for the old *Life* magazine; Odets had been an actor. He had come to the opening of my play *Texas Town* and had been very complimentary. I knew his sister Florence and I asked her, "How does he do it?" "Do what?" she said. "Write plays." "Same as you," she said. "He just writes them." Later she called me up and said, "He listens to a lot of music."

And many years later Terrence McNally was quoted as being even more dependent on music in writing. He said, "I'm unable to begin a play until I've selected a score for it. To a great extent, I learned dramatic structure by listening to music. Classical music is highly structured, and its structure can be successfully mimicked by a playwright. For example, I listened to Bach's *Goldberg Variations*—a little aria with thirty-two variations—while writing *Frankie and Johnnie in the Claire de Lune.*"

I did not see the Group Theatre's first production of Odets' *Awake and Sing,* but I saw its revival several years later. It was a New York play if there ever was one. New York was in a depression and New Yorkers were desperate. The play found a way to speak to them and for them. It is rarely revived today. The dialogue that once seemed fresh and innovative now seems mannered and stilted. And this is true of many of the famous and successful plays of that period: *Tomorrow the World, Watch on the Rhine, Idiot's Delight, The Petrified Forest, Winterset,* and *The Eve of St. Mark.*

Plays, it seems, can speak effectively to one time and place and a decade or two later become lifeless and purposeless. What makes a play transcend time and place and continue to speak vitally to subsequent generations? To my mind, Arthur Miller's *Death of a Salesman* does this, and his *All My Sons* doesn't. Eugene O'Neill's *A Long Day's Journey into Night* certainly does this, and his *The Great God Brown* doesn't.

There were how-to books then, of course. *How's Your Second Act?* by Arthur Hopkins, the producer, had this to say:

> Plays of the future will be more concerned with character than event. This is in line with other art forms as well as with scientific research which is seeking the essence of being rather than dwelling on details of its manifestations. ... Certainly there is a greater and richer variety of expression in character revelation than in the altered application of long used situations. Someone once took the trouble to enumerate the basic situations available to the dramatist. I doubt if anyone would attempt to catalogue the number of character facets that are employable. It would be like counting fingerprints. That the inner man is a richer field than his outer manifestations is evident in much classic literature. One of Hamlet's soliloquies unfolds a more exciting panorama than all of the frantic killings in the last scene.

The Art of Dramatic Writing by Lajos Egri was very popular at the time and full of formulas. Recently I read an article about a teacher of screenwriting. He said, "Egri is the shoulder we are all standing on. This man created the concept of being able to take dramatic principles and lay them down in a book form that really gives information to help the writer." On the other hand I always found Egri's book lifeless and depressing.

Texas Town had been given at the Humphrey Weidman Studio on Sixteenth Street. This was the home base of Doris Humphrey and Charles Weidman. Miss Humphrey was a leading modern dancer and choreographer. We became friends. I attended her classes and watched her rehearsals. She was someone for whom "how to" was no mystery. She was very secure in the technique she had developed as both a dancer and a choreographer. She differed not only in technique but in content from that other great dancer and choreographer, Martha Graham, but they both dismissed ballet as a decadent form.

In the late 1930s, William Saroyan's one-act play *My Heart's in the Highlands*, directed by Robert Lewis, was produced by the Theatre Guild for special matinees and was much admired but only had a brief run. Then came his *The Time of Your Life*, and all of the New York theater was under Saroyan's spell. All the young writers were asking how he wrote, and they were told he paid no attention to plot or structure. He created a mood—How to? How to what? How do you create a mood? It was his secret—no one else seemed to know.

Later, when he published four of his plays, he had this to say:

Like *My Heart's in the Highlands, The Time of Your Life* will very likely take an important place in the development of the new American theatre. I know why, but I am going to leave the full details to the critics, as I believe in the right of every profession to function. In one dimension I shall probably always understand the play better than anybody else, but in another I shall certainly never understand it as fully as critics, professional or amateur.

The first draft was written in six days, in New York, beginning Monday, May 8, 1939, and ending Saturday, May 13. The first title was *The Light Fantastic*. There were to have been six acts, one for each day of work. It turned out that the number of acts was five instead of six. Five or six, however, the idea was to write the play in six days. In the number of days of any worker's week. Writers are workers.

Saroyan made the whole process seem so effortless. He had no real theater credentials. He thumbed his nose at the theater and its conventions. The rumor was that he was writing a play a week—no labor—no sweat—no worrying about construction. How to? Odets' latest play had been dismissed as a failed attempt to copy Saroyan.

The Theatre Guild (Lawrence Langner and Theresa Helburn) had produced *The Time of Your Life,* and at the insistence of my agent and in spite of Tennessee Williams' warning, I enrolled in their class at the New School. I attended one session. They had turned down as producers *Life with Father,* which was one of the great commercial successes of the decade, and the question they posed to the class that day was, If you had been given the script of *Life with Father* would you have produced it?

I was by now taking Tennessee Williams' advice and studying writers I admired. Katherine Anne Porter was one; T. S. Eliot and the playwrights George Kelly and Chekhov were others.

Miss Porter had this to say about writing: "I have always had a fixed notion that a writer should lead a private life and keep silent in so far as writing is concerned and let published works speak for themselves, so, in trying to tell you something of what I think and believe about certain aspects of writing, I speak strictly as an individual and not as the spokesman for one school or the enemy of another."

And there is this from T. S. Eliot's "Four Quartets": "For us, there is only the trying. The rest is not our business."

I continued seeing a great deal of modern dance and studying the techniques of various choreographers. I became friends with the gifted young dancer-choreographer Valerie Bettis. She was very interested in combining words and dance, and she asked me to collaborate with her on a ballet—How to? I had never done anything like that before, but she said we would discover a way together. She was a great proselytizer. She felt that the theater's future was in the use of music, words, and dance, and the realistic play was dead and best forgotten. John Martin, the dance critic of the New York *Times*, had told me that he thought the two greatest dramatists of the day were Martha Graham and Doris Humphrey—neither using a single word.

That spring the American Actors Company produced off Broadway my play *Only the Heart* (a title I hated but I was persuaded to use), and it had gotten very positive press. It had no music, no use of dancers, and it was not in a Saroyan mood, but, I think, was an honest attempt to explore deeply troubling relationships among a group of people.

Luther Green, a fine producer, came to see it and said he would take it to Broadway if Pauline Lord would play the lead. Here was the beginning of a dilemma I have had to face all my life. I like many kinds and forms of theater. Pauline Lord, I thought, and still think, was our greatest actress. Her means were realistic, and silence was often her greatest weapon. Her use of dialogue was instinctive and individual. You were not dazzled by her vocal techniques, nor did she have the use of music and choreography, but what she was able to create on stage had its own poetry.

She read my play and asked to meet with me, and I was thrilled. I thought she could do anything, but she didn't agree. She told me that she liked the play but she was wrong for it and would not serve it properly. She said it with such great conviction that I found myself heartbroken but agreeing.

The American Actors Company had been together five years, and though we had some prestige, we had no money. They were desperate to take my play to Broadway. They asked if I would meet with a producer named Jacques Therre. They said he had an idea about how to enhance the play (playwrights, be very wary of that word, *enhance*) and that if I agreed, he would produce it on Broadway. I agreed to a meeting. He introduced himself as the George Kaufman of Paris. The American George Kaufman was known in New York as a craftsman with the supreme talent of knowing how to make plays work for an audience. He was rich and very successful. How to? Therre had no doubts—like Kaufman he said he could turn anything into a hit. That was and still is a favorite phrase in

New York theater. He has a hit. He doesn't have a hit. Therre's methods may have been successful in Paris, but they didn't work in New York, and the reviewers who had praised my play downtown turned on it savagely and said it had been ruined. Valerie Bettis had gone with me to the opening night, and she did nothing to spare my bruised and wounded feelings. We went to a diner on Eighth Street and talked until about four in the morning—at least she did the talking. She told me once again how I and other writers were wasting our time in the realistic theater and she was glad the play had failed, and now we could begin to help create a new theater. How to?

I wrote a ballet for her called *Daisy Lee* in which she spoke as well as danced. It was given at the New York Y.M.H.A. as part of their dance series, and she kept it in her repertory and toured it extensively.

Through Valerie I met that wise old man of the modern dance, Louie Horst. We became friends, and we talked a lot about musical structure, dance structure, and play structure—about all three he knew a great deal. He said that powerful women like Doris Humphrey, Martha Graham, and Valerie were very seductive. They wanted to change theater and make it in their own image. He urged me to experiment with form as much as I liked but in the meantime to realize that no one, not Graham, not Humphrey, had a final answer.

Howard Lindsay was coauthor of the play *Life with Father*. He had grown up in a theater that had no competition from film and radio. He had worked with some of the great theater managers and producers of his day—Frohman, Belasco, William Brady, and Sam Harris. He called and asked to see me. I met him at his town house in the Village, and he was warm and courteous. He said he loved the theater, and it concerned him that young playwrights of talent were being seduced by Hollywood. "As you know," he said, "I have had many successes, and I would like to share with you two rules that I think are the basis of my success as a playwright. One: Never write a play about anyone you wouldn't care to entertain in your own living room. Two: When I go out of town with a play, I never watch the actors, only the audience."

I have been in the theater now as long, if not longer, than Mr. Lindsay had been at that time. And it seems to me that a great many fine plays would never have been written if they had followed his first rule. And as for the second—I can only say I prefer watching the actors.

Each year, Rita Morgenthau, head of the Neighborhood Playhouse, would commission a playwright to write a play using all the disciplines of the school: acting, music, and dance. She asked if I would like to write one. She said I could direct it and Martha Graham, head of the dance department, would choreograph. I wrote the play and it was accepted. The first days of rehearsal arrived, and in I walked to collaborate on a play of mine with Miss Graham (by this time I was calling her Martha like everyone else). I was twenty-seven then, and I wasn't nervous at all. Today I would be in a panic. It was a remarkable experience. She took my play, added a score by Louie Horst, and turned it inside out. She turned to me one day in rehearsals and said: "Don't let me overdo. I sometimes have a tendency to do that." I sat and watched and learned nothing really except to reaffirm what I already knew, that here was a genius and I was blessed to be in the same room with her. It became, finally, an extraordinary evening in the theater, but to this day I can't tell you what she did or how she did it. But something inside me kept saying, "There are other ways, too." There's Pauline Lord—what's her secret? There's Katherine Anne Porter—what's her secret? And T. S. Eliot, Marianne Moore, Ezra Pound, and William Carlos Williams—what's their secret? How to?

The New York reviewers turned on Saroyan. They decided he didn't know after all how to write a play with a real beginning, middle, and end. He had no second act and third act. It was all mood and to be avoided now. How to?

And in the meantime the New York theater intellectuals had a new hero—Jean Paul Sartre and his play *No Exit*. This was the new theater—everything else was old hat. "Poor Saroyan, poor Odets—passé." Of course there had been *The Glass Menagerie*, but it would have been nothing without Laurette Taylor's performance, and Arthur Miller's *All My Sons* was given importance because of Kazan's production.

Partisan Review, in issue after issue it seemed, had a letter from Paris extolling the virtues of the new French theater and its playwrights. They were particularly enthusiastic about a Paris production of Faulkner's *As I Lay Dying*. Tennessee Williams' *A Streetcar Named Desire* was produced, and it got splendid reviews except from Mary McCarthy in the *Partisan Review*. She trashed it.

Elia Kazan had directed *A Streetcar Named Desire* and, soon after, Arthur Miller's *Death of a Salesman*. The American theater had again found heroes: Williams, Miller, and Kazan. It is interesting that Miller and Williams, though they have been in and out of fashion in the New York theater many times since then, have both managed to be continually produced. England has been consistently loyal to them.

I married, and my wife and I went to Washington, D.C., with Valerie Bettis to teach and produce my plays in a small theater. I continued my experiments with dance and music in Washington for five years and finally felt I had learned all I could. It seemed to me that I was essentially a storyteller and I needed to return to a simpler form that allowed me to tell my stories without theatrical distractions. So I went back to a more realistic style—but is anything in the theater ever really realistic or naturalistic with all the theater conventions we depend on?

There had been many changes in the New York theater and among my friends. Louie Horst was dead and Doris Humphrey had been crippled with arthritis and could no longer dance and seldom choreographed. Valerie Bettis was dancing and starring in a Broadway review with the great Beatrice Lillie. Martha Graham had expanded her company to include men and was at the height of her creative power. Television was beginning, and most of its production was in New York. I was asked by the producer Fred Coe to write plays for his Sunday series, Philco-Goodyear. In those days television was live, which meant, like theater, it could not be stopped once a performance began. Each of the writers he hired had a different vision of the use of television. I wanted to keep it close to theater; Paddy Chayevsky wanted it to go in the direction of film. The necessities of the moment, low budgets, small studios limiting the number and size of sets, made my vision the practical one. I did eight plays for Coe, all really one-act plays, which were later published as one-act plays and continue to be performed as one-acts. However, as the audience grew and the budgets became larger, television gradually left New York and moved to Los Angeles. Tape was invented and it became possible to edit the plays, and consequently, they became more and more imbued with film techniques.

Earlier I had met Stark Young, and he had come to Washington to lecture at our theater. When my wife and I moved back to New York we continued our friendship. He was as knowledgeable about theater and dance as Louie Horst had been.

Stark Young many years earlier had been the theater critic for the New York *Times* but left because he did not like to review a play immediately after seeing it. He went, after the *Times*, to the *New Republic*, where he was the theater critic for many years. He had numerous interests and talents. He was a novelist, an essayist, and the skillful adapter of four of Chekhov's plays. He was a gifted painter and theater director. He was knowledgeable about diverse kinds of theater and dance: the experiments of Meyerhold in Russia, German Expressionism (he did not care much for this), the Chinese theater of Mei Lang Fang (which he adored), the Indian dances of U day Shan Kar. Eleanor Duse was his friend, and he loved and admired Martha Graham as well as Pauline Lord.

He had this to say about theater and playwrights:

> The Golden Day in the theatre would dawn when the dramatist himself directed his play, with actors capable of expressing entirely the meaning he intends, and a designer whose settings and costumes bring the whole event to its final perfection.
>
> This blest occasion would exhibit the creator in the art of the theatre working straight, using one medium directly, as any other artist does, as the painter does, the architect, the musician. But such a day never dawns; and the process by which a piece of theatre art comes into existence is nothing so single or direct. We have first the idea or the matter that is to be expressed in this particular medium that we call the art of the theatre. This medium in turn consists of a number of other mediums that compose it, such as the play, the acting, the decor. And these mediums involve other artists, the actor, the director, the designer, the musician, and depend on them. The art of the theatre is the most complex of all arts.

Most theater people then and now would not agree with this theory of his. The accepted wisdom, then and now, is that the playwright should never direct his own play, because he is too close to it and cannot be objective about its faults and what needs to be fixed in rehearsal. That point will be debated, I guess, forever. Edward Albee directs a great many of his plays. David Mamet, too. In England, Harold Pinter directs his own plays once in a while but often directs the plays of others. Alan Ayckbourn nearly always directs the first production of his plays. Some of my plays I want to direct, some I don't.

Stark Young insisted too there were no final *how tos* in the theater, that there were many varied and equally valuable approaches to the writing and producing of plays, and to insist on one supreme or superior way was foolish and finally defeating. This has been most helpful to remember as each year, it seems, a final approach to writing or acting or directing is announced.

The New York commercial theater meantime was in a panic, and productions were shrinking; theaters were closed and sold for parking lots or office buildings or used for TV shows.

Walter Kerr, in his book *How Not to Write a Play*, claimed that the theater, the commercial theater, would continue to decline and lose audiences to film and television unless we found a way to write plays in the way he suggested. He argued that the theater was losing its audiences because of playwrights' continuing to write watered-down versions of Chekhov and Ibsen, and because of their contempt for their audience. He did not necessarily recommend the great money-makers of the past as present models, but he felt there were lessons to be learned from their ability to attract and please audiences.

Edward Albee had this to say in rebuttal:

> Walter Kerr, the drama critic of the *Herald Tribune*, has, among his many alarming opinions, the theory that the excellence of a new play is determined by its immediate mass appeal. To bolster this theory—a sad one if it is true— Mr. Kerr cites the Greek theatre, where 18,000 people a night would crowd in to see *Oedipus Rex*. Let us say, Mr. Kerr neglects to mention, among many qualifiers, that the Greeks had nothing worse to do. And if we carry Mr. Kerr's idea to its logical and dark end, then the *Grand Canyon Suite* is a better piece of music than Beethoven's last quartet. . . . But the contrary is true, as Mr. Kerr knows, as we all know. The final determination of the value of a work of art is the opinion of an informed and educated people over a long period of time.

Whatever the reason for the decline, the playwrights were usually the first to be blamed. ("Where are our Shakespeares? Our Ibsens? Our Chekhovs? Our O'Neills?") Theater veterans said it was the worst crisis they had ever seen, worse than the dark days of the Great Depression, or the arrival of talking pictures. No one, not even the worst pessimist, could realize then just how drastic and far-reaching the changes would be.

Bertolt Brecht, a refugee from Nazi Germany, had tried all during the Second World War to establish himself as a playwright in America. A great deal was written about his plays, especially by his great champion Eric Bentley, but he was rarely produced. There were great hopes for Charles Laughton's production of Brecht's *Galileo*, but it was a commercial failure.

At the end of the Second World War Brecht returned to Germany and was given a theater of his own by the East German Communist regime. His plays, using German Expressionism and classic Chinese theater techniques, began to gain world attention. He called all this Epic Theatre, and playwrights all over the western world began to study the plays and to try to incorporate his techniques. Finally, New York had a successful Brecht production. It was *The Three-Penny Opera*. It had been first produced in Berlin before the war; here, it was produced off Broadway.

In Europe, Brecht's theater was subsidized by the East German government. He didn't have to worry about the cost of productions or whether his plays made a profit.

London discovered a new playwright—John Osborne. He was writing vividly, if traditionally, about England's working class. And his early plays were produced with some success in New York. He said of his own writing, "Timing is an artistic problem, it is the prime theatrical problem. You can learn it, but it cannot be taught. It must be felt. Things like this—composition, sonata form, the line that is unalterable—there are small victories to be won from them, because these are things that seem worth doing for themselves. If you are any good at all at what you set out to do, you know whether it is good and rely on no one to tell you so. You depend on no one."

In England the National Theatre and the Royal Shakespeare Company were being formed and generous subsidies provided by the government.

American actors, directors, and writers looked on with envy. "How to? How to what? How to have a National Theatre here so we will never have to worry about profits again. It will never work over here. Why? Just because it never will. Why not? Opera is subsidized. Symphonies are. Museums. Why not theater? Never mind. It will never work for theater." And so far it never has.

And in a tiny theater in Paris, Samuel Beckett's *Waiting for Godot* was produced, and it soon had productions all over the world. Of all the plays of its time it was the most admired by thoughtful theater critics.

It has had, I believe, more influence than even Brecht on younger writers. Beckett was and is a difficult model. When understood by the actors and directors involved in the production, his plays can be powerful and disturbing. He has influenced a great many American playwrights, particularly Edward Albee in his later, more abstract style, and in England, obviously Harold Pinter. Brecht was not so conspicuous an influence on American playwriting until the recent plays of Tony Kushner, who happily acknowledges his debt to him. In England he has been much more of an influence.

If the theater was dying on Broadway and off, it was alive and thriving off-off Broadway, in the most unlikely places: basements, coffeehouses, and cafés. This all began only a few years after Mr. Kerr published his despairing book. Instead of names like Theatre Collective and Theatre Union of the thirties, groups called themselves the Living Theatre and the Open Theatre. It was a time of social protest, of defiance, the beginning of the drug culture, not unlike the social protest of the thirties and early forties, but harsher, more violent. Four-letter words never before accepted on the American stage were used with abandon. *MacBird, Vietnam Rock, America Hurrah,* and *The Connection* were the off-Broadway successes of the day. The plays were often abrasive and confrontational and embraced and championed caricature. Certainly Howard Lindsay would never want to entertain the characters from these plays in his living room. The early plays of Sam Shepard and Lanford Wilson were produced in those cafés and coffeehouses. Sam Shepard had written forty plays by the time he was in his mid-thirties. His real ambition, he once said, was to be a rock star. His acknowledged influences were rock and folk music. Lanford Wilson was more conservative and traditional but was equally prolific.

There were new manifestos it seemed almost every day: this was the new theater, down with the old. We older playwrights looked on, at least this one did, with interest, but also with profound bewilderment.

Out of Chicago came the plays of David Mamet, influenced by Harold Pinter, but finally evolving a style of his own. Here was an early sign that serious theater was evolving outside of New York.

The Ford Foundation and other similar institutions were determined to see that theater flourished in all our major cities, not just New York, and they poured in money to make it happen. Unfortunately, too often the money was spent on unwieldy and costly buildings. They also provided grants to minority writers to break, as they said, the stranglehold of the white male playwright. They also gave grants to poets and novelists, encouraging them to try the play form, giving them resident grants to write and work at one of the now many regional theaters.

The *how to*s began to assert themselves those days in strange ways even when not sought after, for many young writers were coming to playwriting without seeing much theater, at least not in comparison to the hours spent watching TV and film. It became a given that film was affecting playwriting much more than theater was affecting screenwriting.

Stark Young had been fond of a one-act play of mine called *Roots in Parched Ground* and suggested I make a full-length play of it. After his death I moved to the New Hampshire woods to work on the play. It finally became a nine-play cycle I called *The Orphans' Home*. To prepare for the writing of the cycle, I read and studied Shakespeare's chronicle plays, especially, *Henry IV,* and Sophocles' *Oedipus* cycle, also O'Neill's *Mourning Becomes Electra* and Arnold Wesker's working-class trilogy. I wrote other plays at the time too and listened to a great deal of music, but plays need productions, and there are no theaters in the New Hampshire woods.

I had done an occasional film assignment to subsidize my playwriting, but I had spent little time in New York for nearly ten years. When I did decide to go back, I found a completely changed world. Half the theaters that were there when I first arrived were torn down, and those left were mostly used by musicals. Not only was Broadway decimated, but the off-off-Broadway movement that had seemed so flourishing and vital had begun its rapid decline.

Herbert Berghoff had a small theater on Bank Street, and he invited me to work with him. He was an extraordinary man. Another refugee from the Nazis, he had an abounding passion for American writing and spent thirty years of his life producing and directing new American plays.

We spent many hours after rehearsals discussing the American theater and its future. I marveled at his resilience and optimism. I knew he had survived many tragic catastrophes—the death of his mother and father in a German concentration camp; his fleeing Germany and the theater he had grown up in—and yet here he was in a small theater on Bank Street determined to do the kind of serious work he felt it was one's duty to do. How to? How to find that kind of courage and strength?

I now found younger playwrights asking me how to, much as I once did Lynn Riggs and Tennessee Williams, but now the questions included: "When you have learned how to write a play, how do you make a living in the theater?" The only honest answer to that question was and is: you don't, or hardly or rarely, any more than poets make a living by their poetry.

There are exceptions, of course (they don't want to hear about Neil Simon—they already know about him), and I usually tell them about Alan Ayckbourn, as prolific as Neil Simon and the most produced playwright in the world. He has spent all his theater life running a theater-in-the-round in Scarborough, England. He directs and produces plays, including at least one of his own each year. As he has written so many plays, they vary, of course, in quality. But at his best, he's extraordinary, both for the seriousness of purpose of his plays (mostly comedies) and for his imaginative use of the techniques of theater. He has a superb ear and his physical imagination is boundless.

The *how to*s to me now also included how to write a screenplay or a television play, a question I never thought of asking all those years ago.

I was interested in the answers Elizabeth Bishop gave to someone who wrote her a how-to letter. Here's what she has to say:

> From what you say, I think perhaps you are actually trying too hard—or reading too much about poetry and not enough poetry. Metrics, etc., are fascinating, but they all came afterwards, obviously. And I always ask my writing classes NOT to read criticism.
>
> Read a lot of poetry—all the time—and not 20th century poetry. Read Herbert, Pope, Tennyson, Coleridge—anything at all almost that's any good, from the past—until you find out what you really like, by yourself. Even if you try to imitate it exactly—it will come out quite different. Then the great poets of our own century—Marianne Moore, Auden, Wallace Stevens—and not just two or three poems each, in anthologies—read ALL of somebody. Then read his or her life, and letters, and so on. (And by all means read Keats's letters.) Then see what happens.
>
> That's really all I can say. It can't be done, apparently, by will power and study alone—or by being "with it"—but I really don't know how poetry gets to be written. There is a mystery and a surprise, and after that a great deal of hard work.

And I encouraged the *how to*s that came to me to read plays: Sophocles, Shakespeare, Molière, Racine, Strindberg, Ibsen, Chekhov, Yeats, Synge, Sean O'Casey, Brecht, Beckett, Williams, Miller, Albee, Lanford Wilson, August Wilson, David Mamet, Sam Shepard, Romulus Linney. And I tried to make clear that with a playwright the search for knowledge can't stop there. As Stark Young says, "The art of the theatre is the most complex of all arts for they include not only the dramatist, but the actor, the director, the designer, and often musicians." The wise playwright will make it his or her business to learn something of all these disciplines.

Recently Frank Rich in the New York *Times* used me as an example of our contemporary theater's problems. He wrote:

> Fifty-four years ago this week a young man from Texas named Horton Foote made his playwriting debut in New York with a drama called *Texas Town*. Brooks Atkinson, the critic of *The Times*, declared it a "feat of magic."
>
> Last week and some 50 plays later, Mr. Foote, now 79, won the Pulitzer

Prize for Drama for *The Young Man from Atlanta*. In the intervening half-century, he has passed through Broadway during its Golden Age—Lillian Gish starred in his *Trip to Bountiful* in 1953—and won two Oscars in Hollywood (for *To Kill a Mockingbird* and *Tender Mercies*). But, incredibly, Mr. Foote is now in some ways back where he started in the theater. Not only is he still writing about the same Texans, but this Pulitzer-winning play, just like *Texas Town*, was staged on a shoestring in a tiny Off Off Broadway playhouse.

To be exact, only 1,700 people saw *The Young Man from Atlanta* during its four weeks at a 75-seat theater in NoHo—fewer than see *Show Boat* in a single night. Though the play received good reviews, no producer moved it to a large home Off Broadway, let alone on, for an extended run—so financially risky has it become to mount a serious drama requiring nine actors in the commercial theater. If Mr. Foote's plays have much to tell audiences about the psychic fissures lying just beneath the surface of middle-class American life in this century, what does it also say about America that playwrights of his stature must now fight to be heard?

I served on the Pulitzer jury that chose Mr. Foote as one of the three drama finalists this year. I am overjoyed that he won. But no prize, however lustrous, should obscure the fact that even he, after a half-century performing feats of theatrical magic, has no guarantee that his work will be staged in our cultural capital.

You would think this host of apparent difficulties would discourage young writers, but it doesn't, of course. They ask their *how to*s and they continue to write plays and believe they will find a way to get productions and find solutions to the problems they and the theater face today, just as I and my contemporaries asked our *how to*s, refused to be defeated by the problems of the theater we first faced, and refuse to be defeated still.

Bloodline in Ink

Ernest J. Gaines

Since I have lived in San Francisco most of my life, I have been asked many times: when will I write a novel or stories about California? I always say that I will write about California after I have written all the Louisiana stuff out of me—which I hope will never happen. I once *tried* to write about California. I was a young man in the fifties when the Beat era was at its apex. I had read Hemingway's *The Sun Also Rises*, and I could see the same thing going on in San Francisco in the fifties that Hemingway had called "a moveable feast" in Paris during the twenties. So I tried the wine parties and going to jazz clubs and sleeping on the floor instead of a bed, but after a while I got a bit tired of it—especially after I got sick on salami and cheese, French bread, mustard, and white wine.

I could see that the bohemian life was not for me, but I wasn't going to let that stop me. I tried writing a novel about an interracial affair with a San Francisco background. San Francisco is a cosmopolitan city and I knew quite a few interracial couples. I worked on this novel for about a year—I think I went through a complete draft—but when I began to reread it, I saw that I was trying to rewrite *Othello*, and I knew that Shakespeare had done it much better more than 350 years earlier. I was also reading stories like "The Turn of the Screw," so I tried to write a ghost story with San Francisco as background. I've told other people that I put it down because it was so real it frightened me. The truth is it never got off the ground. Then I tried to write about my army experience on Guam between the Korean and Vietnamese wars, but after two or three chapters of that I put the manuscript aside. I saw that I was trying to rewrite *Mister Roberts* or *From Here to Eternity*.

In the early sixties many of my colleagues were leaving the United States for Europe, Africa, and Mexico to write their books because America had become too money crazy for them to concentrate on their work. I was supposed to leave the summer of 1962 with a friend and his wife for Guadalajara, Mexico. I had been working on the novel *Catherine Carmier* for three years, but it seemed I was going nowhere. I had written it first from the omniscient perspective, then the first-person and even multiple points of view; I had revised the story many times and changed the title a half-dozen times. Nothing seemed to work for me, and I was convinced that it was because I needed to leave the country. I was working at the post office when my friend and his wife left for Mexico. I told them that I needed to make more money, and I would join them before the end of the year.

But something happened in September of 1962 that would change my life forever: James Meredith enrolled at the University of Mississippi. Every night we watched the news—my family, my friends—and all we talked about was the bravery of this young man. It seemed that whenever we talked about his courage, I felt family and friends looking at me. One night in October or November I wrote to my friends in Mexico: "Dear Jim and Carol, I am sorry, but I will not be joining you. I must go back home to write my book. My best wishes, Ernie." I had already contacted an uncle and aunt in Baton Rouge who had told me that I could come and stay as long as I wanted.

On January 3, 1963, a lady friend of mine drove me to the train station in Oakland, California. Fifty-two hours later I was in Baton Rouge. I had been to Louisiana twice since leaving in 1948, but both times for only a week or two, and both times I lived with folks in the country. This time I would be in the city for six months, and I was determined to live as others did. If that meant demonstration and engagement with the police, then let it be so. But at that time very few civil rights demonstrations were going on in Baton Rouge, and if the police did show up, they stood back and watched but never interfered physically with the gathering.

My Uncle George and Aunt Mamie had a four-bedroom house, where they lived with their nephews and their son Joseph. Each Sunday we would drive out to the country, to the old place where I was born and raised until I left for California. We would visit the old people who would have dinner for us—chicken and greens and rice and beans and a cake and lemonade—and we would all sit there in the kitchen eating. Then I would leave them to walk through the quarter into the field, crossing the rows where the cane had been cut and looking for a stalk of cane that had been left behind. When I found one, I would peel it with my knife and chew it slowly, enjoying the sweetness.

I would look far, far across the naked rows and remember back when my mother and father and the others in the quarter used to work in these fields. Then I would turn and look toward the quarter, back at the cemetery, where my folks had been buried for generations. I would go into the cemetery and look for pecans, and if I found some, I would crack them with my teeth as I had done as a small child. I felt very, very comfortable and safe there because that was where Auntie was buried, the one who had raised me. I did not know the exact place because her grave had not been marked, but I felt more peace in those moments than I had ever felt anytime in California.

On weekdays, back in Baton Rouge, everyone else had left the house for work or school by eight o'clock, and I would have the entire place to myself—me, my pencils, yellow paper, and Royal portable typewriter. That's when I thought of Catherine and Jackson and their families and loves and prejudices, as I rewrote everything that I had written in San Francisco the previous four years. I would work until about three or three-thirty, then put everything away until the next day.

Not long after returning to Louisiana, I was introduced to a group of schoolteachers. In the early evening we would go out to a restaurant to eat and talk. When I was not with this group, I would join my uncle at a local bar with his friends. My uncle worked as a janitor at one of the local oil companies near Baton Rouge; he and his friends were the hard labor-ers, those who did the dirty work. I would join them at the bar and we would have a setup: a pint of whiskey, a bowl of ice, a pitcher of water, and maybe a bottle of 7-Up or Coca-Cola. Each man fixed his own drink. Many times when I reached to get some ice, I would see bits of sand and gravel at the bottom of the bowl. At first I felt some apprehension about using the ice, but when I looked at those guys, they seemed pretty strong. I concluded a little dirt would not kill me either.

Baton Rouge was dry on Sundays, so along with several younger guys, I would go across the Mississippi River into Port Allen and down to the White Eagle. The White Eagle was a tough place where there were always fights, but I wanted to experience it all. One novel, *Of Love and Dust*, and the short story "Three Men" came out of my experiences visiting the White Eagle. I knew now why my novel *Catherine Carmier* was not working for me in San Francisco. I had lost touch with the world I wanted to write about.

I learned a lot about myself and my people those six months that I stayed in Baton Rouge. My most important lesson was that I had not learned very much about either myself or my people from the history books that I had been assigned in California. I had studied literature and learned it well, and I had studied creative writing and learned structure and technique, but the soul of what should have been the novel was still back in Louisiana. Ever since learning that, my approach has been to balance the written word with faces and voices and place.

While attending San Francisco State College in the mid-1950s, I started collecting blues records and inviting friends to my room to listen to the music. Most of my white friends would listen to the records out of curiosity (this was the 1950s, not the 1960s—well before the Rolling Stones made America aware of the value of black blues singers). The white boys and girls in San Francisco would listen to the blues because it was exotic. Very few of my black friends from the college wanted to listen to the blues at all, however. They wanted to forget what those "ignorant Negroes" were singing about. They had come to California to forget those days and those ways.

A lady friend of mine in Washington, D.C., once told me about a young black man who always got in the elevator whistling something from Mozart. I too like Mozart—and Haydn, Bach, Brahms, Schubert, Ravel, and Chopin. I like *Pictures at an Exhibition* by Mussorgsky and "Lark Ascending" by Ralph Vaughan Williams. I like them all. I keep classical music on very low while I'm writing. Though Mozart and Haydn soothe my brain while I write, however, neither can tell me about the great flood of 1927 like Bessie Smith or Big Bill Broonzy can. And neither can describe Angola State Prison in Louisiana as Leadbelly can, or what it means to be bonded out of jail and put on a plantation to work out your time as Lightnin' Hopkins can.

William Faulkner writes over a hundred pages describing the great flood of 1927 in his story "Old Man." Bessie Smith gives us a picture just as true in twelve lines. I am not putting down Faulkner, who is one of my favorite writers. What southern writer has not been influenced by him the last fifty years? What I'm saying to the young black man who found it necessary to whistle Mozart is that there is also some value in whistling Bessie Smith or Leadbelly—a value that I had to discover. Chopin I like very much, especially the nocturnes, but in "Mr. Tim Moore's Farm," Lightnin' Hopkins tells me more about a young man on a southern plantation than Chopin ever could:

> Worse thing this black man ever done
> Moved his wife and family to Mr. Tim Moore's farm.
> Mr. Tim Moore's man [the overseer] never stands and grins.
> Say if you stay out of the graveyard, nigger, I'll keep you out the pen.
> But he will wake you up so early in the morning
> You liable to catch a mule by his hind leg.

After publishing *Catherine Carmier,* my first novel, I tried publishing my *Bloodline* stories. The bloodline in the story is the common experience of all the male characters. I thought the stories—two of which had already been published in journals—were good enough for a book, and so did my editor at Dial Press. But he felt that I needed to write another novel before bringing out the stories. *Catherine Carmier* had sold no more than fifteen hundred copies, which meant no one had heard of the book. And the publishers did not want to take a chance publishing a collection of stories by an unknown writer. "Write a novel," they told me, "and we'll publish both the novel and the collection of stories." "But those stories are good," I said, "they'll make my name." "We know that," they said. "But nobody knows your name now, and we need a novel first."

On the plantation where I grew up in the 1940s there were some tough people and mean people and hardworking people. All the men claimed they could load more cane, plow a better row, outfight, and control their women better than the next man—and most of them claimed more than one woman. When the plantation system changed to sharecropping, many of these people left the plantation for town. There was always some news about them having fights and getting themselves killed or sent to Angola for life.

H. was one of these tough guys. He was tall, very handsome, and tough. He was shot point-blank one night when he tried climbing through a window after hearing that his woman was with another man. Two or three months after this happened, a group of us were over at the White Eagle Bar when one of my friends pointed toward a guy only three tables away from where we were sitting. "That's the fellow killed H.," he said.

"What the hell is he doing here?" I asked. "Shouldn't he be in jail?"

"He was the *good* nigger," my friend said. "You don't have to go to the pen if the good nigger kills a bad nigger. A white man can pay your bond, and you work for him for five years."

I could never get the image out of my mind: this guy sitting there in his blue silk shirt and slacks and two-tone shoes. One day back in San Francisco while I was playing Lightnin' Hopkins' "Mr. Tim Moore's Farm," everything seemed to click for me: Take a guy like this one who killed H. and put him on a plantation under a tough and brutal overseer and see what happens. What happened was *Of Love and Dust*.

I wrote a first draft of the novel in three months and sent it to New York. My editor Bill Decker sent it back to me a month later with this note: "I like the first part of your manuscript and I like the second part of the manuscript, but the two parts have nothing in common. The first part, you have a tragedy; the second part, a farce. Go back and do it one way or the other. Stick to tragedy."

I wrote back: "The state of Louisiana did not take it as a tragedy."

"Too bad for the state of Louisiana," Bill wrote back.

He was right. The first part was serious, and the second part was not. I had thought that if the state of Louisiana could get away with it, why couldn't I? "Your Marcus pulls all kinds of con games on these people on the plantation," Bill said. "And you let him escape?"

"No. He pays. That boy who Marcus killed had a life, after all. And life is valuable."

Three months later I sent the manuscript back. Bill said, "You've improved it ninety percent. Run it through the typewriter one more time and I'll publish it *and* publish your *Bloodline* stories."

Bloodline is the beginning of my going back into the past. I realized after writing *Catherine Carmier* that I had only touched on what I wanted to say about the old place and the people there. My folks, a mixture of black, white, and Indian, had lived in that same parish for four generations before me. My siblings and I were the fifth, and their children the sixth. There were no diaries, journals, letters, or any written words left, but there were the people there who could tell me about my grandparents' grandparents and about the other old people of that time. Some of the stories were horrible, others were funny, but all of them were educational—that other education, the one I did not get out of schoolbooks in California (and I doubt if any students of that time—white or black— got from their textbooks in the South).

Until I went to California in 1948 at the age of fifteen, I had been raised by a lady who never walked a day in her life: my aunt, Miss Augusteen Jefferson. She could not walk, but she did everything for me, my brothers, and my sister. She cooked our food. We brought everything to her at the stove, where she sat on a bench. She washed our clothes. We brought the tub, the washboard, the bar soap, and she sat on the little bench, bracing herself on the rim of the tub while she washed on the board. She patched our clothes when they were torn and disciplined us when we needed disciplining. Of course we had to break our own switch and bring it to her and get down on our knees to take our punishment. Later in the afternoon, after she had her midday nap on the floor, she would crawl over the porch and down to the ground to go into her vegetable garden beside the house. There with her little short-handled hoe she would work among her vegetables: beans, peas, cucumbers, tomatoes, mustard greens, cabbages, whatever she had in the garden that time of year. Other times she would crawl over the backyard to the pecan tree, dragging her little flour or rice sack, and there search for pecans among the grass.

Because my aunt could not go to other people's homes, the old folk would always come to our house, where they would talk and talk and talk all day. When there was no school and I was not needed in the fields, I was kept at the house to serve them coffee or ice water. Not only did I serve drinks, but I also wrote letters for them. (I have been asked many times when I started writing, and for years I have talked about beginning in 1949 in that Andrew Carnegie Library in California, but now that I think back, I realize that I started writing on the plantation sometime around 1945.) And I *had* to be creative, because once the old person said, "Dear Sarah, I am feeling fine, wishing you are the same," it might take the poor soul the rest of the evening to think of another line. If I wanted to go out and play ball or shoot marbles, I had to be able to think of many lines and think of them fast.

After the *Bloodline* stories, I realized that I needed to go farther and farther back in time. *Catherine Carmier, Of Love and Dust*, and *Bloodline* had been easy writing because I had experienced so much of that life myself. But to go farther back would mean research.

Sometime in late 1967, I visited a friend, a professor of English at Southern University in Baton Rouge. As we sat in the living room while his wife prepared dinner in the kitchen, I asked Al, "What was it those old people were talking about when they sat out on the porch day after day and around the fireplace at night? I can remember they talked and talked and talked, but I can't remember what they talked about. You see, I have an idea for a novel about this 110-year-old woman, and the people are going to talk about her, and I want to know what they would have said. The story will take place between 1852 and 1962, from slavery to freedom to the civil rights demonstrations of the sixties. What do you think they would have talked about?"

Al and I started with national events, first with slavery—what the old people had heard from their parents and grandparents. Next we went to Reconstruction—the hard times. We discussed Lincoln, Douglass, and Booker T. Washington because I could remember as a child a photo collage of Lincoln, Douglass, and Washington hanging over the mantel in my aunt's bedroom, just as I would see photo collages of John and Bobby Kennedy and Martin Luther King, Jr., on the walls of other black people in the seventies. We talked about the great national heroes, Jackie Robinson and Joe Louis, then King and the civil rights demonstrators. After national events, we came to state events: the great floods of 1912 and 1927, the cholera epidemic in New Orleans, Huey P. Long and all his men. Next we came to the parish, and we talked about the small town, the parish seat, and the sheriff, as well as the professor who had been killed in 1903 because he tried to teach young black children to read and write and look after their health. (His grave lies on the bank of the river that I described in *The Autobiography of Miss Jane Pittman*. I visit his grave each time I go back to the old place.)

After we discussed the parish, we came to the plantation quarters, where we discussed the crop and the seasons and the work. We talked about the big house, where my grandmother worked for so many years, and the store where the people had to buy their food. We talked about long days, dark nights, little pay, and mean overseers. We talked about a distant sound—the marching of young men and women for civil rights and their spokesman, a young Baptist minister from Georgia.

Al and I must have talked eight or nine hours that evening and into the night, and I still remember the last thing he said to me: that I had a lot of work to do. What he meant was, "This is what they *could* have talked about. Now you have to convince the readers that they did."

I remember that the old people spoke of seasons and not of months. They spoke of cold, cold winters and hot, hot summers when it rained or didn't rain, or when the cane and pecans were plentiful and when they were not. As far as politics was concerned, they could not remember *who* had said something or *when*, but they could tell you *what* had been said and *how* it affected their lives. As a child, I can remember the old people talking about the boll weevils and the great flood. They knew the horror of the flood, they knew how people suffered, they knew how swift the water moved, they could tell you the color of the water, and they could describe the trash and dead animals that the water brought, but they could not tell you what year it had been. I would have to get this information from books; and my main source was Miss Evangeline Lynch, a librarian at Louisiana State University in Baton Rouge.

The first time I visited the library and told Miss Lynch all the information I needed, she said, "My God! Are you sure?" She had heard of me through the *Bloodline* stories and was glad to meet me, but she thought I was taking on a task too big for one person to handle. "Well," she said, "let's start looking around. Most of it should be around here somewhere." In 1972, when I received the Louisiana Library Association Award for *The Autobiography of Miss Jane Pittman*, Miss Evangeline Lynch was in the audience. Twenty-two years later, she was in the audience again when I received that same award for *A Lesson Before Dying*. She was long retired and a bit frail, but she stood and waved again.

Miss Lynch helped me get material from books, periodicals, magazines, and newspapers, but I still had to go to the people. I needed facts, I needed dates, and I got that from the books—from the written words. But I wanted to know how these different events affected lives, and I had to get that from the people.

Mr. Walter Zeno liked his vodka and he liked his wine. Whenever I would come from San Francisco to Baton Rouge, I would rent a car and go out to the old place with one of his favorite bottles. He would squat, not sit, on the porch by the door and drink and talk as I leaned back against a post listening. He had known my grandparents' grandparents and all the others, white and black, who lived on that plantation for the first eighty years of the twentieth century. Either directly or secondhand, he knew everything that had gone on in the parish during that same period. He dated things by season, not by calendar, so I had to go back to

Miss Lynch to find out exactly when events happened. The local things you could not find in books. I have never found any information in book or newspaper about the professor who was killed in 1903, but when you asked the people about him, the braver ones could tell you exactly how the weather was the day he was killed though they could not tell you the year.

I know that I have learned a lot from the works of white writers, and as a matter of fact, I have learned a lot from the works of white European writers such as Turgenev, Chekhov, de Maupassant, Joyce, and others. These were the writers I had to study while a student at San Francisco State in the fifties. I wish that the works of black writers had also been included in the curriculum when I was in school, but none were. I understand all too well the anguish of young people who want to read the works of their own people.

Perhaps that's why I responded as I did several years later, when I was a student at Stanford in the late fifties and my professor Wallace Stegner asked me, "Ernie, who do you write for? Who do you want to read your books?"

"I don't write for any particular group, Mr. Stegner," I said. "I just try to write well and hope that somebody will buy it."

He said, "Suppose someone held a gun to your head and asked you again: Who do you write for?"

"Well," I said, "I probably would say I write for the black youth in the South. I hope that in my writing I can help them find themselves."

"Suppose the gun were still there," he persisted, "and he asked you who else you wish to reach."

My answer was the best I could offer then—or now: "In that case," I told him, "I would have to say I write also for the white youth of the South. To help them see that unless they know their neighbors of 300 years, they know only half of their own history."

Paralipomena to
The Hidden Law

Anthony Hecht

To his friend Alan Ansen, who recorded their conversations, W. H. Auden remarked, "Perhaps my dislike of Brahms is extra-aesthetic, but whenever I hear a particularly obnoxious combination of sounds, I spot it as Brahms and I'm right every time." Now I happen to like Brahms, and I am not alone in this. Nor am I among the musically illiterate in my view. In an essay called "Brahms the Progressive," Arnold Schoenberg wrote, "The sense of logic and economy, and the power of development which builds melodies of such natural fluency, deserve the admiration of every music lover who expects more than sweetness and beauty from music." What is interesting about Auden's anti-Brahms prejudice, and what he merely hints at in his suggestions that it may be "extra-aesthetic," is glossed and explained in Humphrey Carpenter's biography, where it is reported of Auden and his lover Chester Kallman, " . . . he took over wholesale Chester's prejudice against Brahms." This is interesting in that very often people in love, or couples who have shared a life over long years, come to adopt one another's tastes and views. Not uncommonly these are social or political views; but sometimes they are aesthetic tastes as well. Auden's feelings about Brahms probably had less to do with Brahms than with his own domestic life.

Something of the same curious mechanism may be at work in his, to my view, absurd and mistaken ideas about Shakespeare's *Henry IV.* There are a number of essays in which, highly suspiciously, Auden claims that there is no character development in Shakespeare's two-part play. He writes, "Seeking for an explanation of why Falstaff affects us as he does, I find myself compelled to see *Henry IV* as possessing, in addition to its overt meaning, a parabolic significance. Overtly, Falstaff is a Lord of Misrule; parabolically, he is a comic symbol for the supernatural order of Charity as contrasted with the temporal order of Justice symbolized by Henry of Monmouth" (*i.e.,* Prince Hal, later Henry V). It is this typological kind of thinking that allows Auden in one of his poems ("Under Which Lyre") to refer to "the prig Prince Hal." But the real clue to Auden's views of the play very probably may be found in his enthusiastic attitude toward Verdi's *Falstaff* and in one of his essays on opera he flatly asserts that there is no character development in opera. Whether or not this generalization about opera is true (and the libretto of *The Rake's Progress* renders it doubtful), I suspect he has imputed to Shakespeare's play, by a sort of time-warped inference, the same kind of stasis, and one which afflicts most of his own dramatic work. The literary-critical retort to Auden is best supplied in John Dover Wilson's book, *The Fortunes of Falstaff,* where the maturation of Prince Hal, and the concomitant corruption of Falstaff is carefully analyzed; Northrop Frye says much the same thing in *Fools of Time.* But such analysis would very likely have had no effect on Auden, who, by imposing upon the play his notions about the opera, was again exhibiting a symbolic act of loyalty to Chester Kallman, whose devotion to opera was passionate.

Let me turn to what may be some more serious matters. Too late for mention in my book about Auden's poetry, *The Hidden Law,* I made what seems to me an important discovery about some lines in one of Auden's best and most celebrated poems, "In Praise of Limestone," a poem I greatly admire. The lines in question are part of a description of south-Italian landscape:

> The poet,
> Admired for his earnest habit of calling
> The sun the sun, his mind Puzzle, is made uneasy

> By these solid statues which so obviously doubt
> His antimythological myth. . . .

If I had ventured to comment on these lines earlier, I would have assumed that the phrase "the poet" was meant generically, and referred to the foibles of all poets, though perhaps especially to "Romantic" ones, who like to *regard* themselves as poets, and who interpose nothing between the world they observe and their own "creative imaginations." Their "antimythological myth," according to this reading, would be the myth of themselves as the sole creators of everything in their poetry. Had I made this assertion I would have been only fractionally right. I discovered, to my great surprise, that Auden has something far more precise and personal in mind. In a letter written on June 7, 1956, from Cherry Grove on Fire Island to Ursula Niebuhr, the wife of theologian Reinhold Niebuhr, Auden reported, "Have been reading the latest Wallace Stevens; some of it is very good, but it provoked me to the following little short." (It needs to be explained that "short" is Auden's term for a brief, epigrammatic verse comment or obiter dictum of his own.)

> Dear oh dear, more heresy to muzzle.
> No sooner have we buried in peace
> The flighty divinities of Greece
> Than up there pops this barbarian with
> An antimythological myth,
> Calling the sun the sun, his mind *Puzzle.*

Clearly, by "antimythological myth" Auden refers to Stevens' "Supreme Fiction." You can bet that if I had known Ursula Niebuhr's book, *Remembering Reinhold Niebuhr* (in which this letter appears on pp. 288–89), I would certainly have mentioned it. And not only for the light it shed on Auden's views of another poet, but because it also exhibits his characteristic tact in concealing from the general public the fact that what seemed like a generalized disapproval of a literary tendency has behind it a precise individual target.

Now I turn to a still more serious topic. In his commonplace book, *A Certain World,* Auden declares, "Christmas and Easter can be subjects for poetry, but Good Friday, like Auschwitz, cannot. The reality is so horrible, it is not surprising that people should have found it a stumbling block to faith. . . . Poems about Good Friday have, of course, been written, but none of them will do. . . . The 'Stabat Mater,' which sentimentalizes the event, is the first poem of medieval literature which can be called vulgar and 'camp' in the pejorative sense." Now, the "Stabat Mater," an anonymous thirteenth-century poem, is admittedly histrionic in its grief, but Auden's dismissal of it is very curious, coming as it does from one devoted to the campy dramas of grand opera (with their theatrical lamentations), and from one who is the author of an excellent poem about the Crucifixion called "Nones." Moreover, there are many powerful and moving poems about the Crucifixion, as Auden surely knew. Apart from many anonymous ones, including one I quote in my book that begins,

> His body is wrappèd all in wo,
> Hand and fote he may not go.
> Thy son, lady, that thou lovest so
> Naked is nailed upon a tree,

there are many others, including Jacopone da Todi's "De la diversità de contemplazione de croce," and his "Pianto de la madonna de la passione del figlio Iesù Christo," and the far more familiar poem by George Herbert, "The Sacrifice." Why does Auden pretend to ignore all this? Perhaps because he found himself engrossed in a topical controversy surrounding Theodor Adorno's unequivocal assertion: *After Auschwitz there can be no more poetry.* Auden appears to have adopted Adorno's view. It is a view that has been contested by others, including Edmond Jabès, who wrote, "To Adorno's statement that 'after Auschwitz one can no longer write poetry,' inviting global questioning of our culture, I am tempted to answer: yes, one can. And furthermore, one must." The American poet Mark Strand's comment on Adorno's dictum was, "After Auschwitz one can no longer eat lunch, either; but one does."

Another illuminating detail in Auden's poetry appears in a poem called "Precious Five," where Auden addresses what amounts to a prayer to the five senses: smell, hearing, touch, sight, and taste. The prayer is in fact addressed to the organs identified with these senses: the nose, the ears, the hands, the eyes, and the tongue, the last of which is ambiguously identified not merely with taste but with the power of speech. All these organs are enjoined to "behave themselves," to observe a suitable and almost reverent decorum. Each of the senses is reminded of how it can become corrupt, and how it requires discipline. The tongue in particular is specifically reminded of "The old self you become / At any drink or meal, / That animal of taste / And of his twin, your brother, / Unlettered, savage, dumb, / Down there below the waist. . . ." That brother of the tongue,

"Down there below the waist," is the penis. The unlettered, savage, and dumb member of this pair of brothers serves as a warning to the more articulate, civilized, and eloquent brother, the tongue, against heedless impetuosity and the carnal selfishness that takes over when the disciplines of thought and decorum are absent. The "old self" it becomes "at any meal or drink" is the crudely appetitive, infantile self, a baby's or a lust's concern only with immediate satisfaction.

And there is another matter which appears both in Auden's poetry and in his prose. (A number of critics, by the way, have pointed out how often Auden converts insights gained in the humble course of book reviewing into valuable details in his poems. This was true from the very outset of his career.) The poem I now want to address is one of the *Horae Canonicae*, specifically the one called "Sext," the canonical hour celebrated at high noon, and the one that inaugurates the anguish of the Passion and anticipates the ritual hour of the Crucifixion, observed at three in the afternoon, and called "Nones." The first of the three parts of "Sext" goes,

> You need not see what someone is doing
> to know if it is his vocation,
>
> you have only to watch his eyes:
> a cook mixing a sauce, a surgeon
>
> making a primary incision,
> a clerk completing a bill of lading,
>
> wear the same rapt expression,
> forgetting themselves in their function.
>
> How beautiful it is,
> that eye-on-the-object look.
>
> To ignore the appetitive goddesses,
> to desert the formidable shrines
>
> of Rhea, Aphrodite, Demeter, Diana,
> to pray instead to St. Phocas,
>
> St. Barbara, San Saturnino,
> or whoever one's patron is,
>
> that one may be worthy of their mystery,
> what a prodigious step to have taken.

There should be monuments, there should be odes,
to the nameless heroes who took it first,

to the first flaker of flints
who forgot his dinner,

the first collector of sea-shells
to remain celibate.

Where should we be but for them?
Feral still, un-housetrained, still

wandering through forests without
a consonant to our names,

slaves of Dame Kind, lacking
all notion of a city,

and, at this noon, for this death,
there would be no agents.

The commentary on these verses might begin with an observation of the ironic burden of the last lines just quoted, suggesting that humanity had to mature, advance, and sophisticate itself before it was not only worthy of a salvific Crucifixion, but capable of the necessary act of crucifying Christ. It presupposes that the devotions paid to pagan deities must have been qualitatively different from Christian worship, being that Christian worship is putatively *disinterested,* whereas pagan worship is always concerned with personal or communal advantage. The "first flaker of flints" is made the spiritual superior of a worshiper of Demeter, to whom one would pray in hope of an abundant harvest; whereas even though the flint-flaker might be engaged in the manufacture of a weapon to be used for the practical purposes of the hunt, at the moment he is viewed in this poem he is rapt in concentration and has forgotten his dinner. We must elect not to question the claim that Christian worship is purely disinterested, and that none of the saints is ever appealed to for pressing personal reasons. In *The Hidden Law* I quoted some prose of Auden's as a gloss upon his lines, part of an essay called "Pride and Prayer" which appeared in the March 1974 issue of *The Episcopalian,* where he wrote:

As an antidote to Pride, man has been endowed with the capacity for prayer, an activity which is not to be confined to prayer in the narrow religious sense of the word. To pray is to pay attention to, or, shall we say, to "listen" to someone or something other than oneself.

Whenever a man so concentrates his attention—be it on a landscape or a poem or a geometrical problem or an idol or the True God—that he completely forgets his own ego and desires in listening to what the other has to say to him, he is praying.

Choice of attention—to attend to this and ignore that—is to the inner life what choice of action is to the outer. In both cases man is responsible for his choice and must accept the consequences. As Ortega y Gasset said: "Tell me to what you pay attention, and I will tell you who you are." The primary task of the schoolteacher is to teach children, in a secular context, the technique of prayer.

Petitionary prayer is a special case and, of all kinds of prayers, I believe the least important. Our wishes and our desires—to pass an exam, to marry the person we love, to sell our house at a good price—are involuntary and therefore not themselves prayers, even if it is God whom we ask to attend to them. They only become prayers insofar as we believe that God knows better than we whether we should be granted or denied what we ask.

A petition does not become a prayer unless it ends with the words, spoken or unspoken, "Nevertheless, not as I will, but as thou wilt."

What both poem and prose comment present seems to me seriously muddled. And the muddles are of three kinds: historical, theological, and moral. I shall try to address these in order. First of all, historically, the poem invited us to move from the worship of Aphrodite, Demeter, and Diana to the act of addressing prayers to St. Phocas or San Saturnino (there seem to have been at least four of the last-named), and to remark of this change: "what a prodigious step to have taken." The taking of this step presumes an advance—religiously to be sure, but historically as well. The pagan worship clearly predates the Christian. But when, a few lines later, the poem turns in admiration to "the first flaker of flints," and regards him as a nameless hero, we have moved backwards in time to something like *Pithecanthropus erectus,* while still admiring that primitive as somehow superior to pagans in terms of his ability to rise through concentration into selflessness.

Theologically, in his essay Auden acknowledges that petitionary prayers cannot be called wholly disinterested, and in this sense it is only by embracing a specific Christian orthodoxy that they can be called different from, and superior to, the prayers of pagan worshipers. He posits, as though it were proven, that the pagans were incapable of spiritual selfless-ness, a highly debatable position, and one confuted by the figure of Socrates or the philosophy of the Stoics.

It is, however, the moral component of the poem that presents the chief problems. Auden is arguing that man's besetting sin is his self-con-cern, a species of Pride, the most fundamental and universal of the Seven Deadly Sins. (Among his very late apothegms is one that reads in its en-tirety: "Blessed be all metrical rules that forbid automatic responses, force us to have second thoughts, free from the fetters of Self.") This self-regard, this narcissism, whether as selfishness or self-love, is so common a human failing that any escape from it deserves to be remarked upon and applauded. Auden furthermore identified this kind of self-con-sciousness with the inauguration of the romantic period, with which he had a very limited sympathy. I find myself quite willing to assent to the claim that self-concern is a pervasive spiritual flaw, a common form of sinfulness. I would also agree that certain kinds of concentration on ob-jects other than oneself can be wholesome and laudable. It may even be that in writing his poem Auden had in mind Simone Weil's book *Wait-ing for God,* in which she writes, "Training in 'attention' is the essence of prayer." There is, however, another side to the problem which neither of these authors takes into account, but which is examined with great care and attention by Hannah Arendt. She wrote of it as "The Banality of Evil," and by this she meant that bureaucracy tends to manufacture for itself a kind of moral blindness which serves as a self-protective vaccine against any consciousness of its own malfeasances. It permits the bureaucrat, at whatever level he may be stationed, the illusion of moral immunity to any dubious acts he is required to perform. By this means most of the Nazi hierarchy were able to believe that their whole labor consisted of minute attention to impersonal detail, even when this involves the exter-mination of millions. This seems to me a serious, valid, and important objection to Auden's poem and essay.

I want now to add comments on some other works of Auden's. Among the poems, the one beginning "Who stands, the crux left of the watershed," and another beginning, "Perhaps I always knew what they were saying," seem to me more important than most commentaries acknowledge. Were I not too badly to unbalance the proportions of my text, I'd like to examine at some length Auden's brilliant set of lectures on "the Romantic spirit," titled *The Enchafèd Flood.* This seems to me a particularly interesting and important work because of Auden's curiously equivocal stance in regard to the romantic period and its chief poets and authors. Opera, and his assimilated musical tastes, brought him firmly into the romantic camp. But from the outset he was devoted to the sanity, clarity, and balance of the neo-classical poets, and in many personal ways he bore a remarkable resemblance to Dr. Johnson.

I was particularly struck by this in the course of reading Walter Jackson Bate's splendid biography of the great eighteenth-century poet-critic. Consider these striking parallelisms. Both Auden and Johnson had very poor eyesight; both held cleanliness in utter disregard. (About Auden, Stravinsky remarked to Edmund Wilson, "He is the dirtiest man I have ever liked.") Both Auden and Johnson were disposed, in Bate's words, to choose "the wrong side of a debate, because most ingenious, that is to say, most new things, could be said upon it." Both held (again in Bate's words) a "life-long conviction—against which another part of him was forever afterwards to protest—that indolence is open invitation to mental distress and even disintegration, and that to pull ourselves together, through the focus of attention and the discipline of work, is within our power." Both believed that "effort in daily habits—such as rising early—was necessary to 'reclaim imagination' and keep it on an even keel." They shared some views of government and the dangers of tyranny. Bate describes Johnson as "becoming more slovenly in dress and eating habits as he ran about London, [where he] left a train of disarray wherever he entered," and Auden notoriously exhibited the same personal habits. Auden greatly admired the kind of virtue Johnson praised in Robert Levet: "Here was a man," Bate remarks of Levet, "who, despite serious disadvantages, performed a useful and charitable function not impulsively or occasionally but with unwavering constancy. It was an example to frail human nature of what could be done." Both Johnson and Auden were, on principle, indifferent to their surroundings. In addition, Bate writes of Johnson, "he was able to distinguish between 'loving' and 'being loved' and to value the first without demanding equal payment through the latter," while Auden wrote, "If equal affection cannot be, / Let the more loving one be me." Both men were determined, if at all possible, "to be pleased" with their circumstances and with their fellow human beings, as a reproval of their own "impatience and quickness to irritability or despair." Both men repeatedly maintained (again in Bate's words) that "the 'main of life' consists of 'little things'; that happiness or misery is to be found in the accumulation of 'petty' and 'domestic' details, not in 'large' ambitions, which are inevitably self-defeating, and turn to ashes in the mouth. 'Sands make the mountain,' [Johnson] would quote from Edward Young." Both men exhibited an uncommon courtesy and respect for others. Of Auden's considerateness I can myself attest, while Bate writes that, much like Auden's habits in this regard, "Johnson had been making a point for some time of never beginning a conversation but of waiting until someone else spoke to him directly. . . . It was part of his renewed effort to acquire 'good nature'—'easiness of approach,' grace and relaxation, and was an indication that he was not allowing himself to dominate the conversation." Both firmly believed that Fortitude "is not to be found primarily in meeting rare and great occasions. And this was true not only of fortitude but of all the other virtues, including 'good nature.' The real test is in what we do in our daily life, and happiness—such happiness as exists—lies primarily in what we can do with the daily texture of our lives." These resemblances might be carried one extraordinary step further: since both men were by nature disposed to admire neo-classical decorum, and to exhibit it in their work, Johnson's ability to praise the pre-Romantic extravagance of Richard Savage is a precedent for Auden's "Romantic Iconography of the Sea," which is the sub-title of his Page-Barbour Lectures, *The Enchafèd Flood.*

Let me turn to a specific poem of Auden's. It is famous, and among the more popular of his early poems, the pseudo-ballad or folksong called "As I Walked Out One Evening":

> As I walked out one evening,
>   Walking down Bristol Street,
> The crowds upon the pavement
>   Were fields of harvest wheat.
>
> And down by the brimming river
>   I heard a lover sing
> Under an arch of the railway:
>   "Love has no ending.
>
> "I'll love you, dear, I'll love you
>   Till China and Africa meet
> And the river jumps over the mountain
>   And the salmon sing in the street,

"I'll love you till the ocean
    Is folded and hung up to dry
And the seven stars go squawking
    Like geese about the sky.

"The years shall run like rabbits
    For in my arms I hold
The Flower of the Ages,
    And the first love of the world."

But all the clocks in the city
    Began to whirr and chime:
"O let not Time deceive you,
    You cannot conquer Time.

"In the burrows of the Nightmare
    Where Justice naked is,
Time watches from the shadow
    And coughs when you would kiss.

"In headaches and in worry
    Vaguely life leaks away,
And Time will have his fancy
    To-morrow or to-day.

"Into many a green valley
    Drifts the appalling snow;
Time breaks the threaded dances
    And the diver's brilliant bow.

"O plunge your hands in water,
    Plunge them in up to the wrist;
Stare, stare in the basin
    And wonder what you've missed.

"The glacier knocks in the cupboard,
    The desert sighs in the bed,
And the crack in the tea-cup opens
    A lane to the land of the dead.

"Where the beggars raffle the banknotes
    And the Giant is enchanting to Jack,

And the Lily-white boy is a Roarer,
    And Jill goes down on her back.

"O look, look in the mirror,
    O look in your distress;
Life remains a blessing
    Although you cannot bless.

"O stand, stand at the window
    As the tears scald and start;
You shall love your crooked neighbour
    With your crooked heart."

It was late, late in the evening,
    The lovers they were gone;
The clocks had ceased their chiming,
    And the deep river ran on.

The poem features three voices. The first one we may call "the speaker," a master of ceremonies who acts as presenter, the "I" of the poem. To him are assigned the first seven lines, the first two lines of the sixth stanza, in which he introduces the clocks of the city, and the final quatrain. The other two voices are those of the lover and the clocks, to the latter of which is given the largest, most dramatic and ominous part of the poem.

The speaker's introduction to the poem may seem innocent enough, and the line "As I walked out one evening" might recall some opening lines of Elizabethan poetry: Southwell's "As I in hoary winter's night," Richard Barnfield's lyric "As it fell upon a day," or even the American cowboy ballads, "As I walked out in the streets of Laredo," and "As I walked out one morning for pleasure." More apt, I think, might be the children's riddle-poem that begins, "As I was going to St. Ive's," for Auden's poem, as we shall see, is laden with materials from children's folk literature and lore. I must confess that for many years I was unable to read the third and fourth lines about the pavement crowds as harvest wheat without thinking of Eliot's "The readers of the *Boston Evening Transcript* / Sway in the wind like a field of ripe corn." So close was this association in my mind, so strongly did I suspect that Eliot's lines influenced Auden, that I was long misled as to the true significance of Auden's images. (The Eliot poem is very complicated, and far removed from Auden's tone and purposes, but too complex to discuss here.) The speaker goes on in the following lines, in the manner of a comparatively self-effacing m.c., to present the lover.

(I will return at the end to the imagery of the opening lines. The river, of course, is important. It reappears at the end. It is itself a symbol of, among other things, the passage of Time. William Gass, critic, fiction writer, professor of philosophy, who happens to live in St. Louis on the banks of the Mississippi, writes, "To live by a river is to live by an image of Time." And Time, as the clocks in this poem will insist, is a central force of great significance in the poem. But in a way that I think has not properly been noticed.)

Let's turn to the lover. What he presents is both ludicrously hyperbolic and traditional at once. It is a vaunt, a boast, a brag. His declaration of eternal love should strike us as remarkably familiar. There was an entire genre of such boasting, associated first with epic heroes (in Homer as well as other authors) and appropriated by chivalric poets in the name both of their knightly prowess and in praise of the virtue and beauty of their mistresses, and finally in behalf of their undying fealty to those ladies. The medieval tradition carried on well into the Renaissance, and I will offer a little smorgasbord of examples.

> Love's not Time's fool, though rosy lips and cheeks
> Within his bending sickle's compass come;
> Love alters not with his brief hours and weeks,
> But bears it out even to the edge of doom.
>
> Shakespeare, "Sonnet 116"

> Whatever dies, was not mixed equally;
> If our two loves be one, or thou or I
> Love so alike, that none do slacken, none can die.
>
> Donne, "The Good Morrow"

And in the following lines by Petrarch as translated by Thomas Wyatt, the phrase "my master" refers to Love personified.

> What may I do when my master feareth
> But in the field with him to live and die?
> For good is the life ending faithfully.

In his "Amoretti," Spenser could claim that "Our love shall live, and later life renew." And when, in the fourth act of *As You Like It,* Rosalind asks of Orlando how long he will be true to her, he replies, "Forever and a day." These are extravagant declarations, but the experience of love is almost by definition reckless and emphatic, so the literature of love employs hyperbole quite naturally. Orlando is no more guilty of this than Romeo, and when the lover in Auden's poem says his love will continue till "the seven stars go squawking / Like geese about the sky," by the seven stars he means the Pleiades, a group of stars in the constellation Taurus, supposedly fixed in their astronomical positions, from which they could not be budged until the Apocalypse occurs. What the lover says is that he will be true to his love until that precise, terminal moment. Extravagant, but no more than what Othello says regarding his love for Desdemona: "Excellent wretch! Perdition catch my soul / But I do love thee! and when I love thee not, / Chaos is come again." Another instance (many more could be cited) of poetic vaunt may be found in the following "heroic brag" (not in this case associated with fidelity in love) by Thomas D'Urfey, which was set to music by Purcell.

> I'll sail upon the Dog-star,
> And then pursue the morning;
> I'll chase the moon till it be noon,
> But I'll make her leave her horning.
> I'll climb the frosty mountain,
> And there I'll coin the weather;
> I'll tear the rainbow from the sky,
> And tie both ends together;
> The stars pluck from their orbs, too,
> And crowd them in my budget;
> And whether I'm a roaring boy,
> Let all the nations judge it.

(It may be useful at this point to provide a note about the "roaring boy," not least because he turns up in Auden's poem as "a Roarer." The terms were synonymous, and applied to unemployed young men who, having recently been discharged from military service, sustained themselves by terrifying and bullying the civilian population with threats of violence.)

Let me close my little case of samples with one more declaration of undying love, taken from a volume of *Early English Lyrics* edited by E. K. Chambers and F. Sidgwick.

> As the holly groweth green,
> And never changeth hue,
> So am I, ever hath been
> Unto my lady true;

As the holly groweth green
With ivy all alone,
When flowerès can not be seen
And green wood leaves be gone.

Now unto my lady
Promise to her I make,
From all other only
To her I me betake.

Adieu, mine own lady,
Adieu, my speciàl,
Who hath my heart truly,
Be sure, and ever shall!

The point about this pledge of perfect devotion lies not only in the fact that it was a literary convention and a commonplace, but that it is what young men, in the transports of love, often genuinely feel. If your reaction to the poem is tainted with cynicism when you discover that it was written by Henry VIII, and if you go on from that discovery to the unwarranted conclusion that all men in the end are selfish and deceitful brutes who have at heart only their carnal lusts, you would do well to bear in mind what this conclusion implies about the bottomless credulity of the women to whom such verse is addressed. Modern advertisers know exactly what they are doing when they carry out a commercial campaign for a perfume manufacturer with the slogan, "Promise her anything, but give her Arpège!" As for the concluding vaunt of Auden's lover regarding his beloved, and calling her "The Flower of the Ages / And the first love of the world," we may recall the claim of Yeats, in his poem "The Tower" and in regard to Helen of Troy, that "Helen has all human hearts betrayed." And also recall Frost's still more marvelous assertion (in "Never Again Would Birds' Song Be the Same") that in the singing of birds is still to be heard the inflections and lilt of Eve's own voice.

Auden's lover having made his boast and had his say, it is now the turn of all the clocks to speak; and they flatly repudiate the lover. Their declaration that "You cannot conquer Time" is aimed not merely at acts of infidelity or the transience of human passion but at the universal mutability of all things mortal. It is the tolling bell of mortality, and it immediately ushers in "the burrows of the Nightmare." These burrows are the catacombs of the subconscious, and the remainder of the sermon delivered by the clocks is set in this self-accusatory, self-incriminating region. It is the region of Justice: naked, immitigable Justice of the kind Auden, in another poem, calls "The Hidden Law." And when in this poem it is said that "Time watches from the shadow / And coughs when you would kiss," the act of kissing is classed as an indelicate transgression against seemliness, a gaffe or a faux pas. This is to say that one of the most innocent gestures of love is itself condemned—condemned by Time, the grown-up, who has not only been spying and eavesdropping, but by making its presence known (by the approved signal of a cough) will force all lovers to retire in embarrassment and confusion (like Adam and Eve at the discovery of their shameful nakedness) and thus arrest all thoughts of love. Why is love here regarded as indiscreet? In the lines that tell us that "Time will have his fancy / To-morrow or to-day" we recognize a locution that was traditionally applied, not to Time, but to Death, especially in that medieval genre of "The Dance of Death" (written of by John Lydgate, illustrated by Hans Holbein, and the title of one of Auden's earliest works—1933) in which Death is presented as inviting everyone among all the ranks of Mankind to dance with him. This invitation, this fancy, whim, or choice, is always his. The phrase, "to take a fancy to" someone is usually erotic in meaning. It is the theme of "Death and the Maiden." And since everyone must die, Time and Death can be recognized as more or less equivalents, and as soon as we recognize that equation, almost everything that follows in the poem becomes, for all its hallucinatory surrealism, marvelously clarified. We grasp the meaning of the "appalling snow" that drifts (like a pall) into the green valleys of life with its death-like chill, and the interruption of physical graces and pleasures, like the dances and the diver's "brilliant bow." The "crack in the tea-cup," that most trifling of imperfections, is a sign of some great and damning failure that leads to the grave. Self-accused and self-incriminated in this Nightmare, Mankind desperately seeks to cleanse itself—hence the plunging of hands into water. The injunction to "Stare, stare in the basin / And wonder what you've missed" refers ambiguously to what you had expected to receive but were inexplicably cheated of, as well as to how you must somehow unwittingly have taken the wrong turn, having missed some important signal. Images of inexorable fate abound. The glacier is not only cold, but cannot be deflected from its course; the symbolic fruitfulness of the bed is buried under the arid sands of the desert.

The Nightmare becomes a surrealist parody of what we had hoped for, counted upon, above all, led, as children, to expect. Beggars are in control of the banks; Jack, the boy's champion against paternal tyranny, now entertains a questionable sexual interest in one he was supposed heroically to slay; Jill turns prostitute, and the "Lily-white boy" is also borrowed from the realm of children's literature. In this case it is from a "Twelfth-Night" verse (like the "Twelve Days of Christmas") called "I'll Sing You One-O." It includes the line "Seven for the seven stars in the sky," to which Auden has already made reference, and it concludes, "Three, three, the rivals; / Two, two, the lily-white boys, / Dressèd all in green-o; / One is one and all alone, / And evermore shall be so." The scholiasts have determined that the three rivals are the co-equal members of the Trinity; that One is the One God; and that the two lily-white boys are Jesus and John the Baptist. Which one of them becomes this nightmare's "Roarer" is uncertain, but decidedly out of character, as is everything else in this nightmare's hellish and terrifying world.

The last two stanzas given to the clocks are remarkable for their biblical and religious import, and in this they are distinct from most of the rest of the poem. The clocks assert that "Life remains a blessing / Although you cannot bless." From the clocks' point of view, Life may be blessed in its brevity, and, because it is full of misfortune, brevity is its chief merit. But from another biblical point of view, the blessedness of Life derives from the fact that it is a gift of God; and Mankind's inability to confer blessing is an index of its alienation from a once blessed condition. More striking still is the warped, crippled injunction: "You shall love your crooked neighbour / With your crooked heart." This is a deliberately deformed echo of the commandment that appears first in Leviticus (19:18) and is repeated in the New Testament (Mark 12:28–31). In this nightmare world, however, imperfection has maimed everything, including the most noble acts and purposes.

The force and authority that governs all that happens in this poem, the impeachments voiced by all the clocks in the city to confound the lover and his vaunts, are the reprisals of the Justice that began with Mankind's fall from grace in the Garden of Eden, and have continued to torment him ever since. In Eden there was inexplicably both time and no time. There were days and nights, to provide variety and afford occasion for rest as for waking life; but there was no aging, nor any change of season. Milton (in Book IV of *Paradise Lost*) wrote:

> The birds their quire apply; airs, vernal airs,
> Breathing the smell of fields and groves attune

> The trembling leaves, while universal Pan,
> Knit with the Graces and the Hours in dance,
> Led on th'eternal spring.

(264–68)

The timeless world of which the lover sings, and which is envisioned as one in which love will last (in Orlando's words) "forever and a day," the Edenic world yearned for by children, in which the moral order is clear and Good is always triumphant, this world was ruined once and for all by Mankind's act of disobedience which, again in Milton's words, "Brought death into the world, and all our woe."

Now this interpretation may strike some as disputable when applied to the work of a poet who renounced his religious faith in 1922, and counted himself a partisan of the secular and revolutionary forces of the Communist movement. Auden himself has said that until somewhat later in his life (this poem was written in 1937) he believed he had, in his own words, "done with Christianity forever." Nevertheless, even in these years of secular preoccupations, he had written poems that were unambiguously prayers, though it was not always clear to whom they were addressed. "Sir, no man's enemy" is such a prayer, as are several others from the same period. He was, in fact, using the very language, doctrines and symbols that he consciously repudiated.

I think we are now in a better position to understand the imagery that opens and closes the poem, and is spoken by "the speaker." The point is not to interpret the fields of harvest wheat in isolation, though harvest wheat is an apt symbol of universal mortality. Nor should we think of the "brimming river" simply as what William Gass calls "an image of Time." The point of these images, and their effect, is determined by their conjunctions. The fields of harvest wheat are not simply that natural crop itself, but also and at the same time the crowds *upon the pavement.* The river in the second stanza is juxtaposed with *the arch of the railway.* In both cases a residual Edenic pastoralism (the wheat and the river) is linked with urban concrete and industrial technology. The river, which in the opening "brims" and thereby calls attention entirely to its surface, in the final stanza is described as "deep," its surface ignored, its mystery and hidden character emphasized instead. Both the timeless world of the lover and the taintless world of the child are irrevocably gone. And yet we are at all times in the vicinity, not just of the signs and symbols but the true landscape of early, original bliss. The fields of wheat, the river, both remind us—and we are in constant need of such reminding—that despite our offenses, despite our urbanization, our technological "improvements," paved-over grasslands, and emplaced train trestles, life is a gift of the Creator, and continues to remain a blessing.

Robert Frost's Oven Bird

John Hollander

Mythologizing a construction of nature's—an animal, plant, geological formation, moment of process—could be seen as both a desecration and a celebration of pragmatically considered fact. When this goes on in poetry—what Frost called "the renewal of words for ever and ever"—it is accompanied and invigorated by a reciprocal mythologizing, as it were, of the very words used in the poetic process. Literature is full of purely mythological, mostly composite, creatures—phoenix, unicorn, basilisk, chimera, hydra, centaur—as nature is even more full of creatures totally innocent of interpretation—woodchuck, anteater, turbot, Shetland pony, jellyfish, quail.

But then there are the fallen creatures—lion, eagle, ant, grasshopper, barracuda, fox, hyena—that have been infected with signification from Aesop on. It is one of the tasks of poetry to keep renewing the taxonomic class of such creatures, by luring them, unwittingly, into a cage of trope (which of course they are not aware of inhabiting). Such new reconstructions of animals are almost a post-Romantic cottage industry, even as the rehearsal again and again of the traditional ones characterized pre-Romantic emblematic poetry. Significant emblematic readings of previously unread creatures can do the work of reinventing them—I think of Oliver Wendell Holmes's chambered nautilus, for example, as well as animals of Baudelaire and Rilke. I want to reconsider in these pages a well-known instance of such reconstruction in the case of Frost's oven bird.

North American poetry has no living nightingales or skylarks upon which to descant, meditate, rhapsodize, or preach. Our literature inherited a museum of textual ones, from Ovid's Philomela through Milton's almost personally emblematic nightingale, through the more naturalized bird of Coleridge's conversation poem, "The Nightingale," and on to Keats's. John Crowe Ransom's account is more mythic than ornithological:

> Not to these shores she came! this other Thrace,
> Environ barbarous to the royal Attic;
> How could her delicate dirge run democratic,
> Delivered in a cloudless, boundless public place
> To an inordinate race?

A glance at the etiology of the poetic bird would certainly take in the old, blind Milton's later nightingale (not his youthful question-raiser, of whom more later on), who "sings darkling" at the beginning of *Paradise Lost*, Book III. It is answered by Keats ("darkling, I listen") in his nightingale poem. Shelley's skylark, Blake's lark, George Meredith's wonderful "The Lark Ascending" are all daylight's reciprocal poetical birds and poetical surrogates. Even Yeats's aggressively unnatural clockwork golden bird in "Sailing to Byzantium" partakes of the lark-nightingale tradition. But in the transatlantic New World, skylarkless and unnightingaled, another mythologized bird replaced them. There is a sequence of poems—from Richard Lewis's remarkable poem of the 1740s through those of Joseph Rodman Drake, Sidney Lanier, and Walt Whitman—which retrope the skylark-nightingale for American poetry as the mockingbird.

Lewis's "A Journey from Patapsko to Annapolis," telling in Augustan couplets, but from a Thomsonian perspective, of a trip along the eastern shore of Maryland in the 1730s, describes an encounter with a mockingbird. It so allegorizes the creature as the voice of the new-old American imagination that, regardless of the poem itself's remaining largely in oblivion until this century, never again would mockingbirds' song be the same:

> O sweet Musician, thou dost far excell
> The soothing Song of pleasing *Philomel*
> Sweet is her Song, but in few Notes confin'd
> But thine, thou *Mimic* of the feath'ry Kind,
> Runs through all Notes!—Thou only knowst them All,
> At once the *Copy,—and th' Original.*

It is only the anticipation both of Thoreau's echo that is "to some extent, an original sound" and of Frost's "counter-love, original response" in "The Most of It" that is slightly uncanny here. It is almost as if a transcendence of limitation in genres, modes, conventions, styles—the belated not as incapacitated but inspired by its knowledge of what preceded it—were being embodied in an attendant of the Muse of the New.

Lewis's poem prepares the ground for what will be a subsequent tradition. Joseph Rodman Drake's claim in "The Mocking-Bird" (published 1812) for the bird as poet is a bit more plonkingly expository. The interesting southern poet Richard Henry Wilde (1789–1847) refigures the mockingbird in a sonnet. But by and large, the mockingbird of subsequent southern tradition partakes of the sentimental souvenir in the refrain of Stephen Foster's song ("listen to the mock-ing-bird, listen to the mock-ing-bird"). But Sidney Lanier's "The Mocking Bird" ends with a pseudoriddle; the bird having gobbled up a grasshopper, the sonnet weakly inquires, "How may the death of that dull insect be / The life of yon trim Shakspere on the tree?" While Shakespeare can be considered legitimately adduced (given that the bird can say what was both done and dreamed), the fairly empty question embraces what isn't much of a paradox after all.

The greatest and most poetically powerful mockingbird, the male of the pair of "feather'd guests from Alabama," is Whitman's "singer solitary . . . projecting me," the bird singing of its loss to the "outsetting bard," to the "undertone" of the sea, "the savage old mother incessantly crying." The transumption, in "Out of the Cradle Endlessly Rocking" of Keatsian and Shelleyan nightingale and skylark and of earlier poetic mockingbird alike, is a far more profound matter than the mere Americanization of English poetic tradition. The bird is shaken loose from even contingent personification, and extended another, a new, kind of personhood.

It was to the received avian agenda in general that modern poetry felt unable to subscribe. Richard Wilbur spoke for all his twentieth-century precursors in the early 1950s, I believe, saying in "All These Birds" that

> Hawk or heavenly lark or heard-of nightingale,
> Perform upon the kitestrings of our sight
> In a false distance . . . the day and night
> Are full of wingèd words
>   gone rather stale,
>   That nothing is so worn
>   As Philomel's bosom-thorn. . . .

But Wilbur's late-modernist plea for a powerful ornithology to replace empty mythological clichés goes beyond its own strong demands for a demythologizing of what are, imaginatively speaking, stuffed owls. It pleads for tropes of birdhood and avian particularity by showing both the limits and the consequent utility of a biological reductionism:

>   Let us, with glass or gun,
>   Watch (from our clever blinds) the monsters of the sky
>   Dwindle to habit, habitat, and song,
>   And tell the imagination it is wrong
>   Till, lest it be undone,
>   it spin a lie
>   So fresh, so pure, so rare
>   As to possess the air.

But perhaps the essential modern rejection of a trope of birdsong is Wallace Stevens' in "Autumn Refrain," his near-sonnet of 1931—ten years earlier than "Come In." In this poem (about not being able to write anything for two years), grackles lately blathering recall to him the whole avian tradition and its perhaps empty literariness:

>   The yellow moon of words about the nightingale
>   In measureless measures, not a bird for me
>   But the name of a bird and the name of a nameless air
>   I have never—shall never hear. . . .

And he opts out of all of it: the typically bivalent phrase "the evasions of the nightingale" refers both to evading the poetic nightingale issue and to what said nightingale issue itself evades. The poem ultimately finds, as Harold Bloom suggests, some difficult but important "residuum" in the desolate sound of the grackles. There is a great deal to be said of the Stevensian distrust of birdsong, but it is now time to turn to my central text, Frost's powerful and problematic contribution to poetic ornithology, the—in this case, accepted—thrush of "The Oven Bird." The poem invoking it negotiates a remarkable course between a rhetoric of certainty about what a bird is singing/saying/doing and a strong inner sense of its "evasions." And it maintains a very un-Stevensian, albeit parabolic, awareness of natural fact.

First, though, the unpoetic ornithology: *Seiurus aurocapillus,* a ground-walking warbler, is common in deciduous woods; it builds a domed nest on the ground and sings from an exposed perch on the understory. That an American poem addressing—or addressing itself to—this thrushlike bird might consider its ground-built, oven-shaped nest, would seem obvious, with interpretations of some sort of pragmatical sublime—being well-grounded instead of lofty—immediately offering themselves. But the poem we are to consider does not.

THE OVEN BIRD

There is a singer everyone has heard,
Loud, a mid-summer and a mid-wood bird,
Who makes the solid tree trunks sound again.
He says that leaves are old, and that for flowers
Mid-summer is to spring as one to ten.
He says the early petal-fall is past,
When pear and cherry bloom went down in showers
On sunny days a moment overcast;
And comes that other fall we name the fall.
He says the highway dust is over all.
The bird would cease and be as other birds
But that he knows in singing not to sing.
The question that he frames in all but words
Is what to make of a diminished thing.

Robert Frost's sonnet was started in New Hampshire around 1906 but probably finished in England around 1914, far from the shared habitat of bird and poet. Its ending leaves us with a kind of riddle. The opening puzzles us also, slightly, but in a different way: sonnets don't start out with couplets unless they intend to continue—and as they rarely do—with six more of them. But both octave and sestet of this one are initiated by couplets, and in the latter instance, somewhat strangely for other reasons as well. From the outset, too, we notice at once how casual and how problematic its rhetoric is. "A singer everyone has heard"?—come now, people in London who have no more heard that singer than a New Englander could hear a nightingale? No: this is the conventional palaver of nature-writing, of a newspaper feuilleton of the sort that you might still find in a rural newspaper in England (or, more likely, being sent up in a Monty Python routine). But the low-literary, prosaic tone is modulated with a jolt, as the second line declares its ulterior agenda, with a "*Loud,* a mid-*sum*mer and *mid-wood bird*": because of the contrastive stress marking the new coinage "mid-wood," the spatial reciprocal of the ordinary, temporal "mid-summer," the line ends with three stresses (you might call it two overlapping spondees), confirming the opening, intrusive, almost self-descriptive, "Loud."

The bird "makes the solid tree trunks sound again," but at a first reading this always itself sounds strange. It is not just the densely alliterative pattern, first pointed out by Reuben Brower. "Sound again"—have they been unsound? No, not Germanic "sound" (Modern German *gesund*) but French and Latin sonorous "sound"; still, why do we pause momentarily? Do we mistake this bird for a kind of woodpecker, hitting the trunks directly, and thus making them less gesund as they make them resound? But it is this purely English and non-Latin way of putting "resound" that then allows the matter of an echo of a prior sounding—that of the earlier—and perhaps for this poem, ordinary and, despite literary cliché, unpoetic—spring birds, since silent.

Then comes the first of the three reiterated assertions of his asserting: "He says . . ."; it will be apparent later why it is not the seventeenth–eighteenth-century locution, the transitive "he sings," or its version in the nineteenth century and later, "he sings of [whatever it is]." What "He says" first is hardly celebratory, but pragmatically observational, quite this side of sounding dirge-like.

The next thing he says is more interpretive, at first reminding us of the dropping of spring blossoms and of how we tend to read these as nothing more dire than the end of a particularly gorgeous overture or prelude, but then letting the resonance of the term "petal-fall" linger on—as if to make us think, *yes, they do fall, don't they?* We half notice, too, the phonological patterning here, in which one dactylic foot embracing a hyphenated compound is echoed by another on another (unhyphenated) one: ". . . early [*petal-*fall] is past / When pear and [*cherry* bloom]. . . ." But woven across this is an alliterative pattern, in which *petal, past,* and *pear* enact a different kind of connection, followed by the analogous but more potently expressive assonance of "went *down* in *show*ers." Yet this line is not end-stopped here but flows into the phonologically plain "On sunny days a moment overcast." But there is another mode of resonance at work, one of word rather than of word-sound. There is a subtle aroma of nuance here: the leaves are cast under, in—and for—a moment, even as the sky is momentarily overcast; the point isn't loudly made or brandished triumphantly but allowed wonderfully to happen.

But then things become problematic again. *Who* says "And comes that other fall we name the fall"? This line is all the more complex and problematic here because it initiates the sestet, and we want the full stop at the end to be a comma, as if to say, "When fall—that other fall—comes, he says [with respect to that] that the highway dust is covering everything." The normal grammar would be that of "come the fall" ("come Sunday," etc.); the present third-person singular verb form here suggests a counterthrusting inversion ("And [then] comes that other fall"). But the first reading would also reaffirm syntactically a linkage that the couplet rhyme (again, in an anomalous place for a sonnet) is implying. Yet the couplet is broken. And we are reminded by the disjunction that the covering of highway dust—the stasis in between petal-fall, which initiates fullness of leaf, and leaf-fall, which initiates bareness of branch—is midsummer stuff, and we can't have the syntax the way we'd like to. As for the coming of the *real* fall (the "early petal-fall" is the "other"), we'd needed the oven bird to point out to us that it was a version of the primary one, a shadowy type of the truth of autumn (and, by Miltonic extension, the autumnal "fall" as type of the Fall from Paradise, the original one we name the Fall, which brought about the remodeling of Paradise into Nature, fracturing spring from fall, promise from conditional fulfillment).

Relations between literal and figurative falling are made even more interesting by the fact that in the Romance part of English, "cause" and "case" are based ultimately on *cadere,* as in the Germanic part we still have residues of the earlier usage "it fell" for "it happened." There are all those other falls, too. (I'm not sure whether the poem's relative reticence on this question keeps them at a safe distance or not—or is there any safe distance from the Fall?) Richard Poirier remarks of this moment in the poem that "any falling—of leaves, of snow, of man . . . can be redeemed by loving, and the sign of this redemption is, for Frost, the sound of the voice working within the sounds of poetry." Certainly, the cadential full stop at the end of this line makes us momentarily more aware of the working of the poet's voice. But in any case, the peculiar one-line sentence, which makes us keep wanting to open it out into a dependent clause and a full couplet with a comma, gives us meditative pause. Perhaps it works as something of a springboard *pour mieux sauter* into a final quatrain, which—in sonnet form—can seem itself to initiate a moment of (at least structural) renewal.

Some of that quatrain's complexity emerges in a straightforward paradox: what does it mean *not* to sing in singing? Well, if the "singing" birds do herald and celebrate spring and the morning—or, as with swallows, fill the sky with skitterish evening hymns—then the oven bird's repeated disyllabic utterance is not that. "He says," "he says," "he says," "he knows," "he frames" (and here, another kind of figurativeness in the trope of material construction); we call the sounds birds make singing, but this bird demands that we suspend the overtones of the word "sing." His are not songs, but propositions: the very subtle rhythm of the line makes this clear, for, in order for the rhyming syllables to be sufficiently stressed, it must go not as "in singing not to sing," as the intoning of the paradox seems to demand, but rather "in singing not to *sing*"—not to be claimed by allegorizing human attention as music, but instead as speculative discourse.

By this point in the poem, the casual older fiction of birdsong—like that of wind in the trees sighing and brooks babbling—cannot be acknowledged. So it is that he frames a question "in all but words," a formulation that is rhetorically quite reticent (birds don't *really* talk, of course, but . . .). The very grammar of the phrase "knows in singing" is unusually resonant: (1) as has been suggested, the bird knows—while singing—not to "*sing*," but rather discursively to raise questions; (2) the bird knows not to sing (literally) in-and-by singing (figuratively); (3) is it as if knowing-in-singing were like Sidney's "loving in truth," a kind of knowing in singing, or as if singing were itself a kind of mental process here? In any event, this song is a matter of knowledge, not of charm, of sense making a claim on *tra-la-la:* I think here—regarding the issue, always crucial for Frost, of the sound of making sense—of how great jazz musicians would often play their purely instrumental solos *to the words,* singing the text (with a complex system of rhythm all its own) internally, in order properly to inform the inventions of the melody alone. In the oven bird's case, perhaps, we implicitly reject "frames in all but music"—birdsong being only figuratively that—and leap over any literal musical agenda even as a poet's *cano* means "I write."

It could also be observed that this sonnet itself, like so many of the other poems in *Mountain Interval*, "knows in singing not to sing." This is not in the way of Yeats's "Words for Music Perhaps" (a phrase which in its way defines all lyric poetry in English from Wyatt and Surrey on); this is more of an implicit revisionary construction of the lyrical of high modernism and may in some ways anticipate the rejection of the thrush's musical pseudoinvitation in Frost's poem "Come In."

Be that as may be, we come to the oven bird's question itself, which may indeed be two questions. Our colloquial phrase "to make [something] of X" can mean to reshape it, use it as material for some new Y, etc. But to ask, "What do you make of X?" means "How do you explain, analyze, interpret X?"—"What's with X?" These strangely paired meanings are those of *to construct* and *to construe.* They both come from the same Latin verb (and are indeed, with unfortunate consequences about fifteen years ago, both designated by the same French word, *construire*). The first of the bird's implied questions, then, is that of what to do with something residual—in this case, summer, but by implication life itself: we are *nel mezzo del cammin* here—something diminished by half. How shall we live the rest of our summer?

The oven bird does not celebrate spring, whether cheerfully, or even problematically, like the cuckoo of *Love's Labors Lost;* it does not pierce the night, in cheerful lieu of illumination, like the winter owl paired with it at the end of that same play. It is neither skylark, singing invisibly at the height of the day, nor the alternatively invisible nightingale. It talks neither of beginnings nor endings, but of a time that is both, in a Janus-like July, looking back and forward at once to an original and a final fall. Midpoints are strange, and they tend not to generate the ceremonies that beginnings and endings do. Midsummer in England tends to mean the solstice, June 21 or thereabouts. But that is not what he celebrates. We tend to think of our northeastern American "midsummer" as somewhere around July 30 or so, and this is the oven bird's time, a somewhat indiscernible *middle* (rather than a clearly marked *center*).

And thus the bird's other possible question points toward and away from this matter: "What to make of"—how to construe, understand, interpret—the residual? Is the bottle of summer half full or half empty?

The invitation to consider the question is not that of the ordinary, crackpot realist cynical put-down of epistemology. I think that the invited discourse on the question, and what it would mean about you and summer to answer it either way, would lie along a line of pragmatic approaches to questioning somewhere between William James and later Wittgenstein. Poirier looks at the question from the point of view of the imaginative energies it generates, referring to "the creative tension between a persistent rising and a natural falling—a poise of creativity in the face of threatened diminishments."

Another way of putting this suggests that one of these diminishments might be thought of as that of the prior tradition itself—Richard Wilbur's "wingèd words / gone rather stale"; and in that kind of subsequent allegorizing that strong poems tend to exude, one thing to make of *that* diminished thing is, by means of newly animated words, "The Oven Bird" itself. And then, as is the case with very powerful and deep poetic ambiguities, the invitation extends to considering the relation between the two kinds of *making of,* between construing and constructing, in which representation is creation, and understandings are imagined: this relation is poetry's realm (as it may not be philosophy's, despite the woodpecker hammering at such a suggestion of the kind of institutional construing recently called deconstruction). And finally, we observe how the line itself ("what to make of a diminished thing") sings its way into the reader's attention with its assonantal *dimin*ished th*ing* that itself diminishes the accentual and thereby the rhetorical weight thrust upon the word "thing" by being put in terminal rhyming position (not "di*mini*shed thing" but "di*mini*shed *thing*").

The way in which the oven bird—"as other birds," too—got to speak, learned what we might call not his sing-song but his say-song—and his way of framing questions "in all but words"—are also part of Frost's concern. Virgil invents what Ruskin would call the pathetic fallacy in his very first eclogue, in which the shepherd Tityrus, *lentus in umbra*—at ease in the shade—*formosam resonare doces Amaryllida silvas*—teaches the woods to resound with the name of his girlfriend Amaryllis and thereby teaches nature to talk poetically to us for the first time.

Another one of Frost's great sonnets, "Never Again Would Birds' Song Be the Same," tells its own etiological story of how birds got to talk, and it is worth considering here for a moment in its relation to the oven bird poem. (A much weaker earlier poem, "The Aim Was Song," propounds another version of such an etiology.) That story involves the imprinting of a human "tone of meaning, but without the words" onto birdsong, an added "oversound" (perhaps as Frost's revision of the ambiguous post-Spenserian word "under-song"). The "he" of the opening line ("He would declare and could himself believe") frames the fiction that Eve's voice, "When call or laughter carried it aloft," added to previously unmeaning birdsong "Her tone of meaning but without the words." That "he" seems to be both Adam and a poet (writing, and then possibly even "believing," his myth). The oven bird's question obviously comes along fairly late in the development of avian discourse. A linkage perhaps more than trivial with the earlier sonnet can also be found in the much more dramatic use of the broken—here, final—couplet. The poem looks at first to conclude with a "bottom line," as it were, the consequential reiteration of the title: "Never again would birds' song be the same." But then, after the full stop, comes the carefully intoned afterthought: "And to do that to birds was why she came" (leaving the implicit question, "To do exactly *what* to birds, by the way? to teach them? infect them? trope them? what?" resonating after this second ending).

I should like to return to one comment from the *Field Guide to North American Birds* that I omitted when quoting from it earlier in this discussion. The oven bird's song is characterized as "a loud and clear *teacher* repeated about 10 times, louder and louder." (It has been argued that, since the oven bird, like many others, also produces a different, high-flying song for a time in spring, the poem is either suppressing discussion of this with a rhetorical strategy of its own, or repressing it. I believe that neither of these is the case and that the lesser-known fact is not, in this instance, to be considered as being deployed in the poem—either for the fact of early, youthful spring-song versus sober, didactic middle-age or, more complicatedly, for the fact of its being very little known.) Like many good teachers of certain kinds, his lesson goes far beyond what "he says," into parable and into questions about questioning. As a poetic fiction of a teaching bird, he seems to be a very guarded, transumptive revision of a particular earlier one, Wordsworth's throstle in "The Tables Turned":

> He, too, is no mean preacher;
> Come forth into the light of things,
> Let nature be your teacher.

The last of these lines is rather awkward in its sound: the near-rhyming, echoic relation of *nature/teacher* is so out of character for the language of poems from *Lyrical Ballads* like "We Are Seven," "Expostulation and Reply," and this one that it feels inadvertent and out of control. This awkwardness casts modern doubt on the authenticity of the quoted expostulation. Thus all birds—even pulpited ones—are not true teachers, and I must note in closing how Frost's bird again recalls a subtradition—but a less diminished one—of poems that consider not merely eloquent but questioning birds. The young Milton's first sonnet was on the nightingale, and what to make of it: for the young, poetically ambitious, virginal poet, was the bird's song a call to attend to a muse or a lover? Was it about sex or poetry? The poem ends with this question, the bird in question in this case involving Milton's nightingale knowing in singing not to say.

W. H. Auden, in a poem of 1950 called "Their Lonely Betters," not only denies the possibility of figurative discourse in birdsong, but in the final stanza invokes Frost, with perhaps the ulterior implication that he is the sort of poet who continues to ascribe words to birds, at least:

> Let them leave language to their lonely betters
> Who count some days and long for certain letters;
> We, too, make noises when we laugh or weep:
> Words are for those with promises to keep.

But within the natural history of poetry, birds seem to have learned to put questions—at any rhetorical level—fairly late in poetic history. Frost's oven bird, is not a universal, but a local singer, framing a question of which you can make a number of things. He is not, like Minerva's owl, an emblem of wisdom but rather an instance of acquiring wisdom— "doing philosophy" in the parlance of Anglo-American analytic philosophers rather than standing for it. As a poetic bird, he is an American poet-teacher. And the teacher-poet who makes a poem out of him is fully able to acknowledge that. There are all sorts of complex attitudes—let alone whatever it had come to make of Eve's "call or laughter"—that must be gleaned from modern birdsong. And yet it sometimes sounds as if the song of the threshold—the qualifications, retractions, considerations, economies of the powerfully unsystematic—can only be philosophy.

Starting In

Diane Johnson

I often wonder whether Norman Mailer's observation that "Experience when it cannot be communicated to another must wither within and be worse than lost" might be true only for writers. Perhaps only writers suffer the paradox that experience must be communicated to be felt. But because we are writers, we all understand the unsatisfied feeling, both full and hungry, inchoate and specific, tormenting and yet alluring—the feeling of wanting to write. Like an itch, like being thirsty, it just comes over you; you feel like writing something. Nonwriters apparently do not feel this need at all.

But the question is always, write what? This question does not automatically have an answer any more than a hunger pang comes complete with a slice of chocolate cake. I am particularly concerned with the limbo between longing and cake because at the moment I myself am wandering in this limbo, this void—the beginning of a novel might be like the void, before the big bang, when preplanetary gases were aswirl, formless but potential, thick with matter and promise, and capable of quite arbitrary possibilities to congeal. At the moment, I am experiencing that tumult of novelistic impressions not yet congealed into form. In other words, I'm planning to write a novel.

We all will have tried launching out immediately on a project, borne by the enthusiasms, only to sink. From this we learn that a work of art must have a plan. If you've written a novel, you probably wrote it, the first time, with relatively little planning—I know I did—because you didn't know the pitfalls lying in wait. For me, though I'm always eager to start right in writing, the time of planning, the wariness with which I hope to avoid those pitfalls, extends with each novel. Nothing is more amusing than having a two-year project in the company of people who interest you, a preoccupation that will inform your everyday life—for your life is affected as you lead it by what happens at your writing table. But you don't want to succumb to the pitfalls; you want to be borne through those inevitable longueurs by your faith in the blueprint. So the first trick sometimes involves the self-denial of not letting yourself start till the blueprint is drawn.

In some ways the work you do in your head or in your notebook, before you begin to write, is the hardest part of creation. For a novel, what you think about can be helpfully divided into familiar categories: the subject, the plot, choosing the narrative method (person and distance), the outline, and the person of the writer herself; how do we stand in our novels? But of course this schema disguises the fact that these issues swirl around together in the mind and have to be dissected out like a yarn tangle. In order to illustrate this untangling process, I'll be making specific reference to the novel I am planning now, that is, to my problems with it, and I hope you will bear with my struggle.

The subject of a work of art, I take it, is not entirely a matter of choice—our subject comes to us, though perhaps incoherently, in bits and pieces. It is ours alone, as personal as DNA, imprinted with our genes and life history. We are stuck with it, up to a point. Our subject is the product of our nature, our experiences, our interests so integrally that it is almost determined despite ourselves.

This isn't to say we won't be caught by a newspaper item, or the experience of a friend—but this is determined too, because what catches us are things that give us a means of dramatizing our inner concerns. Of course, sometimes we want to write *contre coeur*—want to be funny if we aren't, or dramatic and moving if we are funny. I think we always need to try to stretch out of ourselves, change directions, experiment, but what you write always turns out to be like something you, and only you, would write. And it is also true that you can know only so much about your subject until you begin writing, for writing is a process of self-discovery. It's the old saying: how can I know what I think till I see what I say?

It's an uncertain process of knowing as much as you can in advance. For this new novel, I know I'd like to keep on with France, where my last novel was set, and with some of the characters in my last novel, for I didn't feel quite done with them. It must be the feeling Anthony Trollope had once he found himself in Barchester of not wanting to leave. But I know I would also like to put in a woman I'll call Crystal, a woman who took care of my elderly mother, and her cousin Jerry, and their libertarian militia in Oregon, because the novel is to be about, somehow, privileged, sophisticated European life led by Americans there, and the reality of poor, desperate Americans in Oregon, up from Texas, whose minds are filled with old-fashioned, strange fundamentalisms and modern notions about exercise and TV. I have a feeling the Oregonians and the people in Paris will announce their connection if I turn them loose, and certainly I am not getting any closer to understanding them by staring at the blank page. But there are decisions to be made before I can begin to animate them.

I would say—it is often said—the most difficult decision in how to tell the story will be between the first and third person. We'll talk more about that, but meantime, we can't decide between first and third person until we know something general about the structure of the novel. Is it Dickensian—loose and baggy, with subplots and many characters? Or is it taut and formal? This is another place I'm stuck with respect to my current artistic problem. I long for both at once. My taste inclines to the taut and formal novels that unfold in one day, say, or novellas, but I suspect that the material I have in mind dictates episodic and large, which is harder for me. And obviously I have to decide between baggy and neat before I can decide who tells the story. A single narrator—an "I"—can watch a tense, unfolding action; but an elaborate, long novel will require being in the minds of several characters. A loose and baggy story can be told from many points of view. A single first-person narrator can impose structure.

Structure is the element where one feels the ghost of Henry James, and his disapproval of forbears like Dostoevski. It was Dostoevski who said, "I never can control my material. Whenever I write a novel I crowd it up with a lot of separate stories and episodes: therefore the whole lacks proportion and harmony. I have allowed myself to be transported by poetic enthusiasm, and have undertaken an idea to which my strength was not equal." Anthony Trollope said, "There should be no episodes in a novel," but he usually found himself in the situation of Dostoevski. James would surely have agreed with Trollope and did say, "Form alone takes, and holds, and preserves substance—saves it from a welter of verbiage that we swim in as in a sea of tasteless tepid pudding." So, if we are to avoid drowning in tepid pudding, the structure deserves considerable forethought. I tend to think that with me in France and Crystal in Oregon, my novel is going to have to be baggy.

For me, thinking of a structure takes the form of outlines, or diagrams, or even pictures—ways of formally representing the action. I became convinced about the usefulness of the outline after working with several film makers. I still have pinned up on my wall Stanley Kubrick's outline, or rather laying-out, of his film *The Shining*—it consists of nine circles set into two boxes, with the relative proportions of time they will take indicated at the side and the themes and season written in the circles. The reclusive great writer in Don DeLillo's novel *Mao II* has on his workroom wall "the plan of his missing book in the form of lopsided boxes and felt-tipped scrawls and sets of directional signs like arrows scratched out by a child with a pencil in his fist."

Not that you can entirely foresee what will happen, or the ways in which your characters will take on lives of their own. You will come to understand the novel better only in the writing of it. But you can plan a provisional structure, and this plan is a great crutch to lean on on the days you feel stiff or blank. I think that most of the many novels that people begin and abandon are abandoned not because they weren't good or even great ideas, but because they lacked structure. It's hard enough with a structure.

I have always found it an interesting exercise to outline great novels, rather as musicians read scores for delight, or as others read paperbacks. It is an elaborate task and maybe it's make-work, like pencil sharpening, putting off the moment of work—but I find it fascinating, and it helps me to understand how such things as suspense operate, or the order in which narrative elements are revealed, or steps in the character development. I've made very elaborate outlines of several favorite novels—it can take a week of close study and the inventing of symbols to designate main character, or comic relief, or subsidiary themes. This process at least has helped me to understand those novels better: *The Good Soldier, Pride and Prejudice, The Great Gatsby,* and recently *The Thirty-Nine Steps,* which turns out to be very simply constructed indeed. I have learned a lot from these novels, though this may not be evident in my work.

I think I first understood that novels are three dimensional, have a kind of spatial form, when I read Mark Shorer's introduction to *Pride and Prejudice,* which he describes as having a double-diamond shape. I have also profited from rereading an interesting review (which I can no longer find) by Charles Rosen of a book about the musical imagination that describes how the composer holds the themes in mind, suspended or deployed for the length of a symphony, the way a novelist does. Chess is another metaphor for a long work of fiction. All this is to say that inspirational reading is part of the planning process.

I like to hold off deciding who is going to tell the story of a novel until I do some work on the outline or form, in hopes the answer will emerge— one character will be in a better position than others to tell it. I know this is why I've been stuck in the case of my new novel—I haven't worked enough on the structure to see who should tell it. I know five of the characters: There is an American woman married to a famous director living in France. I regret her name, Janet, which I thoughtlessly gave her when she came in, in a minor role, in my novel *Le Divorce.* There's the director, Serge Cray. There is Daisy, a young woman from Oregon, who comes to Paris with a fellow antique dealer—I can't decide on his name—who is involved in something mysterious. There are also the people off in Oregon—the care-giver fundamentalist, Crystal, and the old woman she is caring for, who is the mother of Janet, the director's wife.

Obviously, as I said before, it's a big structural problem that some of the characters are in Oregon, the rest in France. Of course there's the airplane and the fax machine. Or I could abandon France, but that's where I live at the moment, and I want to write more about it. I could abandon Oregon, but I feel that these two halves are relevant to each other, so I'll just have to overcome the lack of unity of place. Somehow. I hope.

You have to know the subject to know the structure. To work on the structure requires you to know something about the plot—this underrated component of all great literature. Plot: the sequence of events, causally related. Modernist writers like Gertrude Stein, E. M. Forster, even Bellow, believed that we shouldn't read for what happens next. Of course, that is why we do read, or one of the reasons. I've written elsewhere in defense of plot as a respectable element of narrative, but to abridge my theory, I believe it came to be despised as an unforeseen consequence of Freud's influence, which led people to think of character analysis—often reduced to a recitation of early traumas—as the only foundation of motivation in fiction, and the only thing of interest, with mere events seeming to be gratuitous manipulation by the writer. From the reader's point of view, we need a plot—and there are important psychological reasons for that, as explained by Aristotle and many people since. Plot, style (another given), and authority are elements that fiction has somehow been losing. By authority I mean, who is the "I" in my novel? or where am I in my novel?

I know some things about my plot and structure. The structure will have some kind of bifurcation or alternation, Europe and America. But it's also meant to be about Serge's struggle with, or for, art. And it's got a scam—an Oregon antique dealer trying to fence a stolen manuscript, which would dictate the lineal pace of a thriller. This dealer—Tony? Daniel?—will spend some of the novel in jail, trying to avoid extradition, because he's afraid of the FBI. The FBI is involved in something shady in Oregon—ah—a connection! Perhaps some of the swirling elements have begun to harden.

Plot is vexing, but bound up with it, the first and maybe hardest choice the writer has to make when she starts her novel is whether to tell it in the first or third person. We all know the advantages of each form. The first person is engaging, intimate, allows the writer to skip around in the narrative with the logic or illogic of psychology, not being bound like the orderly third-person narrator to plod from event to event in rough chronological order. The first-person narrator is free. The third-person allows the narrator to look in at any window, to peer into corners where the "I" cannot have been, to skip over oceans, to pry into the secrets of several minds. But she is bound by certain conventions, and restricted to a more distant, less immediate, magisterial tone.

In the first person, we talk to the reader in our own voice, or a voice we make up, in each case talking directly, intimately. As readers we like this mode because we like confidences, we like hearing people's secrets. Does Janet or Crystal have better secrets? Could I sustain Crystal's redneck voice if I told the novel from her point of view? Or the mother's? Or Daniel's—for that's his name, in jail in Versailles. A first-person voice has a veracity (however spurious), an intensity the third person has trouble emulating. In the first person we can reveal more of our real self or our fictional self, and if self-revelation is our aim, it is the best way to do it, telling our own story in our own words. Europeans say American friendliness is our disguise, our candor a mask behind which, because we omit knowable social rites, we are unknowable. The first person, with its confidential, natural tone and indifference to plot, can mask us also.

On the other hand, as a way to tell a story, the limitations of the first person are well known. They are geographical, we could say. If I, Janet, am here in Paris, I could not have been in Oregon, so how could I have known what Crystal said to mother? Everything I recount must have been told to me, seen with my own eyes, filtered through my own consciousness, and will be colored by that. First person is good for detective stories, where the reader knows only as much as the detective knows, clues they discover together. It's bad for certain kinds of complex ironies that depend on the reader's knowing what different sets of characters are doing or thinking at the same time, and it limits the reader to only one consciousness, the narrator's. Henry James, as we know, chose a path between the first and third person by adopting the limitations of one consciousness as in first person put in the third person—the so-called limited omniscience of his technique.

The first person is limited too if I don't have much of a story to tell. Here is a problem, whether we call it a modern problem or an American problem. I was in Prague a few summers ago while the PEN congress was going on. There were books and authors everywhere, from everywhere in the world, and what struck me was that books and authors in much or most of the world have political significance and a vitality that American writing, overwhelmingly first-person accounts of experiences less than politically or geopolitically or spiritually or morally significant, conspicuously lacks. To put it another way, American accounts of pain and suffering have a slightly meretricious ring in the context of recent European or Asian or Latin American or Rwandan events and political upheavals. Others have something to write about that we really don't. I could use myself as an example. I used to wonder how I could ever become a writer—my parents had been nice, and we weren't Jewish or southern, two categories that dominated first-person novels when I was starting out writing. Instead I grew up in a small midwestern city, insulated from war, poverty, and ghettos, from racial strife, social malice, certainly from massacre and genocide. Apart from an occasional small disappointment or my dog's being run over, what bad thing has happened to me? I am rich and fortunate. Sometimes I think that the increasingly shrill, thrill-seeking excesses of American narrative now, our liking for the surreal, grotesque, or metafictional, is the recourse of writers who have refused to face this basic fact that while Americans (disadvantaged minorities excepted) have to face the metaphysical questions of death and being as much as anyone, they don't have to face them in the same immediate form as, let us say, a person living in Bujumbura today, and this has a vitiating effect on narrative that we attempt to redress with sensational self-revelation.

We usually don't have much of a personal story, but the first person is good when you do have an exciting story to tell of something that happened to you. Huck Finn had an exciting story to tell. Or if things happened to others and you saw them happen. Or even were told about them. Seeing them happen is perhaps the best use of the first person—Nick Carraway seeing what happened to Gatsby and Daisy, or Ishmael on the *Pequod.* When the first-person narrator is not emotionally involved, his skills as witness and interpreter are sharpest, and the reader is saved from long passages of subjective complaint and self-analysis. (In my novel, this would seem to argue for Janet as narrator.) Jane Eyre, telling her own story, though she is usually clear-sighted and brave, has passages that seem to us now a little self-indulgent, and she is a marvel of self-control compared to moderns who have learned their skills of confession on the psychoanalyst's couch.

Edmund White says that he writes in the first person from a sense of political engagement. As a gay writer, involved from the first with the movement to bring gay literature out, he felt he had a duty as witness, and he had experiences to tell about, and he writes wonderfully about all this, but, as he says, he begins to sense the limitations of always writing about one's own experience directly—of course we all do it all the time indirectly. You get bored with your own story eventually. Or should. Probably you can only tell it once with deep conviction and emotion; you can rework it a time or two in other forms. But then? White wrote a biography of Genet, a third-person novel, essays, other things, to get away from the first person. Some people never do get away from the autobiographical and become sort of trapped, as was said of Ralph Ellison, and is said all the time about Philip Roth.

Henry James didn't like the first person because, it would seem, he was not terribly interested in the story of his own life—didn't find much drama there, was too busy writing and dining and sightseeing and visiting and leading the calm life of a sociable gentleman in easy and civilized circumstances. It is too easy to imagine James's writing in the modern confessional mode. There's the fraternal rivalry, the bitter and slightly mad sister, the pain of his sexual ambiguity; above all there is the mysterious wound. What an affecting account he could have written.

Alas, or perhaps luckily, he was interested in others, in their moral dilemmas, and in the way that how they lived revealed the times, the moral and political climate of certain societies. James was a social novelist of a sort that we aren't used to now. To some extent we have to bear in mind the habits of mind of American readers. Again, if I may use my own work as an example, in that I think of myself as a novelist of manners, or of politics, I have written novels about revolution in Iran, racial tension in America, the politics and ethical dilemmas of medicine, the aftermath of Vietnam protest. At least I think of these as the subjects of novels that have been taken—such are the expectations raised by genre and the fact that I am a woman—as cries of protest from the feminine heart, female madness, protest of the woman's lot, and so on. This tendency to assume that women only write autobiographically put me off the first person after *The Shadow Knows,* a first-person novel about, I thought, black people in a housing project, was taken to be an affecting rendition of female paranoia—the narrator's—that is, mine.

That taught me that at least you had better put a little distance between yourself the writer and the reader, to avoid getting him too interested in you and less in the story you have to tell. People became interested in the narrator of *The Shadow Knows,* N, she was called, for narrator—so little did she for me exist except as a teller of the stories of Ev and Osella and AJ. I did invent a little love story for N, a lover who never comes into the novel, and I put in a few little children to tie N down a bit and explain why she was living in the housing development, and these were enough troubles to unleash the powerful magic of sympathy. N got all the sympathy, with little left over for poor Ev, my real heroine, who is knocked on the head in the laundry room and killed.

I have to admit I've just finished a first-person novel now, *Le Divorce.* The narrator is telling the story of her sister's marriage in France. This narrator, named Isabel after James's heroine Isabel Archer, has never been abroad before and sees Europe through very Californian eyes. She makes cultural comparisons: "I gradually came to understand that Monsieur Cosset was religious, at least officially, and believed in God and the Catholic religion, in a not preoccupied but nonetheless solid way. At first I was shocked by this. At home, you wouldn't go out with anyone openly religious, because in California mentioning God, only done by ministers and congressmen, automatically symbolizes hypocrite." And so on. I think to tell the same story in the third person would have been to sacrifice Isabel's ability to make such frank evaluations about Americans and the French, whether you agree with her or not. First person makes the sex scenes harder, though. First person bedroom scenes are apt to be clumsy and embarrassing. "Then he put his hand there," or "there." "I took off my pantyhose." It's odd that many famous porn novels, like *Fanny Hill*, are first-person accounts, ostensibly by women, though written by men.

First person is a good choice for writers who don't have an important, wrought, descriptive literary style. A person talking is not convincing if he speaks in too elaborate or poetic a way. Some very talented writers can manage a conversational and at the same time highly descriptive style. E. L. Doctorow's *Billy Bathgate* is a wonderful example of an accomplished style that doesn't sacrifice the intimacy and pace of speech: "This plump little man with a tapemeasure hanging around his neck like a prayer shawl perhaps he had reason to know of the pride of poor people." The run-on sentence is ostensibly because Billy is semiliterate, though with remarkable eloquence, and telling everything pell-mell in a way that would seem affectation if it were the author using the same words. "I liked the big-bladed silent ceiling fans turning slowly as befitted the dignity of the diners," Billy tells us. It's interesting that most of the great first-person accounts are put into the mouths of young people like Billy, or Huck, or Jane Eyre. The implication—and the fact—seems to be that the freshness of perception of a young or naïve person permits him or her to recount aspects of experience that the reader ostensibly knows but likes to hear about again, remembering the first time he himself saw those turning ceiling fans at Schrafft's.

We know that Huck Finn is not Mark Twain and Billy is not E. L. Doctorow. Sometimes, though, the reader assumes or is told in some way that the writer and the first-person narrator are one but that the work is not an autobiography; that is, it hasn't committed itself to entire literal truthfulness to history. *Autofiction* is the word the French use for a form somewhere between truth and the kind of distilled truth to the essence of existence, if not to the chronology, that is fiction. We've been calling it "creative nonfiction." Again, the familiar example of *Jane Eyre*, which had much in it that was taken from Charlotte Brontë's life and added some wishful thinking and genre conventions—Mr. Rochester, the mad wife, the gloomy mansion, and so on. It is worth mentioning that an author will usually be taken for one of his characters, and this is especially true for women writers, as if they were deficient in imagination. What was true for Charlotte Brontë is still true. People assumed, even before they knew her identity, that Jane Eyre's tale was true, and when they learned the author was a woman, people criticized the violence and immorality of this modest little person from a country parsonage.

Writing in an autobiographical mode invites the reader into your real life, to like or to criticize you. A subtle difference in intention becomes evident. Some writers want their readers' responses to carry over into real life. Lillian Hellman was a writer whose memoirs were extravagantly admired, and she was someone who greatly enjoyed in her real life the admiration she had earned for the brave heroine Julia, or the self who stood up to the House Un-American Activities Committee—she wrote those memoirs from a writerly impulse to witness but also perhaps for the pleasure of being a real-life heroine to her readers, a sort of social secondary gain.

The danger, which she found out to her cost, is that the writer of an autobiography is pledged to a truthful account, and readers are outraged at the least little distortion of a fact that would not bother them if changed in a fictional account. Hellman was greatly criticized when people realized she had not told everything just as it happened but more as she wished it had happened, hopes mixed in with facts, inconveniences left out. Hellman wrote about staying in a hotel during the Spanish Civil War. She speaks of remembering Martha Gellhorn, the second wife of Hemingway, wearing pretty clothes and claims there was a sort of pass that didn't come off, from Hemingway. Martha Gellhorn wrote indignantly in the *Paris Review* that none of this could have happened. Controversy raged, rage and controversy that could have been avoided by the discreet words, "a fiction," appended to *Pentimento,* Hellman's book. A mysterious ire surrounded Hellman that would not have been directed to a modest novelist who made no claims to truth, or one who latched on to the new vogue for "literary nonfiction."

Most often, a first-person account has the ring of autobiography and is very near to autobiography, but the author has rearranged events into a more meaningful, concise, affecting design, the components of his own experience. Literary nonfiction. One has to be a little careful of the tone. How much self-pitying the reader will find acceptable is a delicate and maybe a regional or familial or ethnic thing. Someone formed as I was in stiff-backed midwestern stoicism can feel rather embarrassed by too much self-pity openly expressed; in some cultures or families the eloquent recitation of one's woes is expected and admired—indeed demanded, with anything less being deemed cold and withdrawn. The very disapproving term *self-pity,* current in families like mine, may not even be in use in others.

The point is that writing in the first person about one's own woes invites the word *self-pity.* and can exhaust the reader's patience. Brenda Uland quotes Dostoevski's mockery (in *The Possessed*) of the sort of writer who says, describing a shipwreck: "What are the sea, the storm, the rocks, the splinters of wrecked ships to you? I have described all that sufficiently to you with my mighty pen. Why look at that drowned woman with the dead child in her dead arms? Look rather at *me,* see how I was unable to bear that sight and turned away from it. Here I stood with my back to it, here I was horrified and could not bring myself to look; I blinked my eyes,—isn't that interesting?"

Clearly it might be better, in the first person, to write about someone else's misery, or pretend to, while your personal story, if it must, elliptically forms around the edges.

Much depends on the convention adopted by the first-person narrative, which brings us back, as always, to structure. Is the story being written down after the events? Is it being spoken? Is it a letter to someone else (which implies a dialogue, for the writer can be expected to anticipate the response of a recipient he knows, rather as in the critical theories of Bakhtin)? Is it a journal? Harry Mathews' recent *The Journalist,* a man writing in his journal, shows us some of the advantages of that form. The diary writer can use shorthand to himself. He can ruminate, speculate: "So will writing down memories extend ordinariness to the 'dark' past, or merely orderliness? Someday my world will be filled with plain things and people. . . . Transport. 3.00, Rest. 19.50, Books 38.00. Trying only ½ lorazepam." Shorthand that tells us he took a bus, went to a restaurant, bought some books, hasn't been sleeping well.

The first person can serve as a way of reassuring the reader of the truth of farfetched events. If "I" tell you I found this manuscript in a trunk, or was told this tale by a stranger, you will believe me, and it, sooner than you believe a story that starts right out asserting a plague-ridden city in North Africa in an unspecified era.

Of course, issues of reliability come up with the third person too, but in general, the narrator is automatically reliable. The actual author is not automatically reliable, because the reader brings to the reading what he knows of the writer's personal history, obsessions, etc., whether he, the writer, likes it or not. Reading, say, a Mailer scene of marital strife, every reader remembers the famous stabbing incident. As with the first person, sex affects reliability—women are considered less reliable than men, especially women of sexually active age—distracted, romantic, creatures of emotion, victims, mad, etc. Old women become reliable again, believed to have achieved wisdom—honorary men. Age affects reliability. Old is wise. Young equals naïve freshness, whose misunderstandings yield fresh perspectives, a kind of gifted naïveté in itself reliable, revealing an ulterior truth. Male narrators are more apt to be thought of as reliable at any age, though if they are young they may be subject to the same fallibility issues as female characters are.

But at this point you are already saying, impatiently, that all this analysis is too calculating and intellectual and will douse the creative spark. Certainly we must not let our calculations show in the work. The American novel is anti-intellectual almost by definition, except when written by foreigners, like Nabokov, say. When *Pale Fire* was published, American readers were thrilled to find that a novel could be a poem and a puzzle with erudition and clues. But they wouldn't want it every day, and they don't write that way. We tend to write myth and romance, updated, of course, and we tend to write in genres, which are a form of the mythic, and we at least for a period since the fifties have written subjective, even lyric novels. Perhaps it is time to find out what kind of novel you are writing.

Have I come any closer to deciding how to tell my story of Janet, Daisy, and Crystal? Maybe. I know a few more details than before. If I say them over to myself at night, maybe I'll dream the way to begin. Sometimes you must plunge in before you are ready—this is the paradox, the Catch-22 of art. Like a squirrel in a cage, you spin in a circle: you can't know subject till you know structure and vice versa. You can't know either till you know something of the plot, and you can't work on plot till you know who tells the story, which you can't know till you know the subject. But the Catch-22 of art means that even without knowing everything about what you are going to write, you have to begin, and then of course your trouble begins. But having done a little work beforehand, you are forearmed, at least partly, and hope to have a heartier appetite for the struggle.

A literary critic must be prepared to say, "This is good,
though I don't know why; not yet anyhow"; indeed his
more formative opinions are nearly always like that.
—William Empson

Benign Obscurity

Donald Justice

The basic notion is probably less novel than I want it to be, and I may be
behind the times to think that it has anything new about it. But I suppose everyone would agree that in the normal course of going through
poems we put up with a good deal of obscurity, and with oddly little com-
plaining; and I think this merits some attention, if not concern. I hope I
will not be seen as joining the very popular revolt against reason and good
sense if I suggest that there is in fact something to be said for obscurity in
some of its simpler forms. It can at the very least be a sign of the presence of something hidden, of something perhaps too difficult to express
without resistance.

It often seems to me that others have seen and understood a poem
more quickly than I have done, certainly more thoroughly. Yet I hardly
think that this deprives me of the influx of pleasure a reader is entitled
to expect from a good poem. Mine may or may not be a feeling different
from what other readers, perhaps luckier than I, experience; it seems
to me as deep and as secure. It even seems that whatever I do see and

understand at first glance, so to speak, is crucial, perhaps the most important aspect of the reading experience, though it obviously can only be incomplete and partial. Eliot speaks of having been "passionately fond of certain French poetry long before [he] could have translated two verses of it correctly"; and even if you have not had precisely this experience, you have probably found that liking a poem very frequently precedes understanding it.

When reading a poem for the first time you cannot really expect to be sure of what the meaning is. Whether the uncertainty lies with you or with the poet or in what ratio the blame is to be apportioned would vary from case to case. I must suppose that most poets, even if they do not make it their constant aim to say everything with the utmost clarity, still do not go much out of their way on purpose to prevent understanding. It would be only the self-consciously experimental poet who might do this, and for that reason we may leave the experimental poet out of our study. For I like to think that all the best poets are capable of thinking and thinking straight, and probably intend to do so most of the time, although they do not always manage to stick to the plan.

Of course some uncertainty can remain even after repeated readings, that is, if the poem has about it a certain amount of the complexity we like to think makes it worthwhile. But unless the poem has seized you in some powerful way, you will not want to take the trouble of trying to worry out its meaning later. The kinds of obscurity I am thinking about are common enough, and one kind in particular seems to occur with considerable frequency in the work of a certain type of poet. Hopkins, Hart Crane, Dylan Thomas: these would be among the obvious examples. Even if the sense is never wholly grasped, poems that work like theirs may in spite of that go on exerting some inexplicable hold, if this is not too embarrassing an admission to make. I am trying to describe what actually happens when we read rather than what, according to one theory or another, ought more respectably to happen.

The singular power of such poems seems to penetrate the emotional system directly, without ever having to pass through the understanding; or at least the understanding, with its analytical tendencies, is temporarily suspended. The effect can be like a sharp, small blow or a sudden breath of wind. As I say, it is perfectly possible to go on admiring such poems without altogether understanding them. I would compare the experience to reading a piece of music at sight. I happen to be a good sight reader, and the average piece of piano music I can usually manage to play through, not without mistakes of course, but about as well on the first try as after many run-throughs, for my technique is not very sound. Just so with a poem—repeated readings may never get rid of all the mistakes, but you can, from the outset, get a very good idea of the way it goes.

Nor is any commentary, any gloss, ever likely to answer all questions completely; it seems that the first uncertainty is going to remain as part of the overall effect. Psychologically the uncertainty itself could probably be said to constitute at least a small part of what manages to get communicated, just as it was a part of the original excitement. A sense that some meaning hides behind the curtain of language is almost enough to satisfy one provisionally, especially at an early stage of reading. It probably matters less than you would think just what the meaning proves to be in the long run, if you ever do get at it. But believing or guessing that a meaning of some kind is there is important, I think, for all good readers. One of my contemporaries has been quoted as saying there are no hidden meanings in his poems, a remarkable confession. If this were true, the poems would most likely end up as trivial or frivolous, and there would be no obscurities at all. I do not mean to argue that the reverse would hold true; obscurity in itself can hardly guarantee importance and seriousness to a poem.

But I am one of those who like poetry that is difficult, up to a point. It engages more of the whole being; I am bound to it by more ties of association. One is encouraged to go on trying to get beyond the difficulty by a kind of confidence the poem arouses, probably because it looks carefully put together; or it looks brilliant and flashy; or it reminds one of previously admired poems and thus through resemblance borrows some of the authority of other work. I want to give the name of *benign obscurity* to this kind of difficulty, for there are plenty of other kinds that do not work this way but only leave one feeling rather lost and helpless. Notes help with such poems, despite the prejudice in some quarters against notes, as if poetry could be the better for not making an effort to be understood. There may even be a touch of truth in this attitude, for the mysterious admittedly has some pull to it, though in the end I think one is better off for being given the odd fact. Though sometimes mistaken for it, obscurity is not the path to the sublime; but then in fairness you must add that neither does it defeat the sublime.

I mentioned Hopkins earlier. Hopkins can be very difficult, protesting all the while that he aims at being "intelligible." In his case, the very oddities of the surface are enough to make the poems look at least as obscure as they are, and anyhow oddness itself strikes me as a minor variant of obscurity. There are passages in Hopkins, many of them, that come at you first as a sort of golden shower of words, attached presumptively to some plot or argument it is clearly going to take a good deal of labor to work out, a labor the beauty of the text teases you into postponing, perhaps indefinitely. We have, for the time being, hardly more than a rich helping of almost pure language, and the truth is probably that we are not displeased by that. We may feel dazzled, overwhelmed, a bit dizzy, as from drinking too deeply. We may not want the dazzle to end up as the total message, but style can slide over into content and nudge it out of the way. Nor is this altogether a bad thing, at least temporarily. Poetry would seem a dull and ordinary kind of expression if the possibility of the poet's being carried away did not sometimes hover over the text as one read.

Hopkins does go overboard, I think, in "Spelt from Sybil's Leaves" with extraordinary results. Almost before beginning to worry about the possibility of there being a meaning, one senses the great power of the poem; at least I did, when first encountering it in late adolescence; and some of that first charmed bewilderment still clings to the poem when I read it now:

Earnest, earthless, equal, attuneable, | vaulty, voluminous, . . . stupendous
Evening strains to be time's vást, | womb-of-all, home-of-all, hearse-of-all
    night.
Her fond yellow hornlight wound to the west, | her wild hollow hoarlight
    hung to the height
Waste; her earliest stars, earl-stars, | stárs principal, overbend us,
Fíre-féaturing heaven. For earth | her being has unbound, her dapple is at
    an end, as-
tray or aswarm, all throughther, in throngs; | self ín self steepèd and
    páshed—qúite
Disremembering, dísmémbering | áll now. Heart, you round me right
With: Óur évening is over us; óur night | whélms, whélms, ánd will end us.
Only the beak-leaved boughs dragonish | damask the tool-smooth bleak
    light; black,
Ever so black on it. Óur tale, O óur oracle! | Lét life, wáned, ah lét life wind
Off hér once skéined stained véined varíety | upon, áll on two spóols; párt,
    pen, páck

Now her áll in twó flocks, twó folds—black, white; | right, wrong; reckon
    but, reck but, mind
But thése two; wáre of a wórld where bút these | twó tell, each off the other;
    of a rack
Where, selfwrung, selfstrung, sheathe- and shelterless | thóughts agaínst
    thoughts ín groans grínd.

I have to believe that the first impression this poem makes must involve, as it did for me, being overwhelmed by the language of it prior to any determined attempt to get at the meaning—the language and, yes, the rhythm, which must strike anyone as not only different from the general run of poetic rhythm but quite singular and personal, vaguely Anglo-Saxon perhaps, but strangely outside of history. Still, the rhythm cannot be said to have very much to do with the plain sense of the poem, if this poem can be said to have anything about it so ordinary as a plain sense. What I am calling its language consists not only of a special diction, featuring a dialect word like *throughther,* a coinage like *attuneable,* and several typical Hopkins compounds, but a variety of sound effects, chiefly alliteration and a Welsh-like chiming, together with various twists of rhyme, all of which being piled together make for a very mannered kind of writing, just the sort you would instinctively turn away from if there were not in all this seeming chaos some feeling that it was not chaos after all; and not mere decoration and design either, though decoration and design are certainly a noticeable part of the working of these words, words that would otherwise appear to have been rolled out of the word-box like so many dice. The atmosphere, all gloom and doom, rises up out of the poem early in any reading of it, never to depart; and this seems to be enough to give you the idea that all the bits and pieces of language and rhythm you are hearing can be connected, if not so much to one another in any familiar or logical way, then perhaps by referring them all loosely back to some general mood-center. There is undeniably an emotional as well as a verbal harmony to the whole. With the accumulation of detail, the evening—the atmosphere and mood associated with the evening—deepens, deepens seriously. One becomes aware in the last part of the poem that some type of judging is to take place; things are to be divided into good and bad, light and dark. You see that it is a kind of judgment day, perhaps the very day of judgment itself. Whether it is just a case of the day's gloom bringing on a state of depression or whether this is indeed meant to stand for the last day of all, the feeling could hardly be more oppressive and at the same time full of awe, thrilled and exalted, an odd complex of emotional responses.

Whatever theology was in it for Hopkins is probably not necessary for a reader now to work up in any detail, although I would not deny that the more the reader knows the fuller his sense of the poem becomes. I am saying just that you need not start at that end of it. It was doubtless a good thing for the author to know more than we do and for him to put as much as he could of what he knew into the poem. We are aware of the theology without, most of us, wishing to become converts, as one of Hopkins' editors is said to have done. No doubt the Jesuit reader who has the kind of feel for language and rhythm I like to think I have would do better by the poem than I could hope to do; at the same time, a Jesuit reader, lacking this equipment, would not do as well as I suppose I might. This is to say that a good part not only of the value but of the very substance and life of the poem does not depend primarily on what passes for meaning. The string of alliterations in the first line makes that point early, so that you know from the start what you are letting yourself in for. The choice of this run of adjectives is determined as much by sound, by the fact that they alliterate, as by their descriptive or doctrinal point. If there had been another halfway appropriate adjective alliterating on *v* (*vast* must be saved for the following line), we might not have got the famous musical rest between *voluminous* and *stupendous* in the second half of the line. Hopkins was obviously so much in love with the jingle-jangle of poetry that I cannot see him choosing to rest the case on meaning alone. This is one poem in which (to use I. A. Richards' very useful old terms) the vehicle has wrestled with the tenor—and won.

I hope I shall not be classed as some sort of philistine for making the argument, but as Empson remarks, "one must judge how far a thing needs explaining"; and I am trying to avoid the kind of critical thinking that pretends to understand more than is there to be understood and that at the same time is unwilling to state the obvious, especially if it would seem in any way naïve to do so. The truth is that obscurity, in the actual transaction between writer and reader, is not altogether destructive, despite the hard line taken against it by responsible critics. We act on this principle every day in reading even if we are sometimes reluctant to acknowledge it. By obscurity I do not of course mean the blanketing fog that can creep over everything. It ought to be admitted, all the same, that one may be led on by precisely one's failure to grasp what is being said.

And there is the excitement, meanwhile, of being in beyond one's depth.

A poem like Hopkins' sonnet could be glossed much more closely and narrowly than I have attempted to do. It is the kind of poem that tempts you to gloss it to death, for that matter. But I believe that what makes it so powerful is involved less with the specifics than with something broader, more general; there may be as much theology in it as there is human feeling, but what comes across is the human feeling.

And then of course a poem or a passage in a poem may still be obscure even after the critic has told you what it means. For one thing, the critic may be wrong about it or partly wrong. For another, it is likely that he has managed to dig out only by hard labor the sense that had lain darkly hidden. Some part of the effect may always be a lingering memory of the very darkness in which it was hidden, or just the fact that at one time it had seemed to be hidden. Hart Crane even more than Hopkins gives you this impression over and over again—the very difficulty and the attendant puzzlement are an essential part of the whole package, and you do want the whole package.

So far I have been concentrating on the highly charged deployment of language that leads to a shift of attention away from the plain meaning of the poem to the strong and sometimes strange sounds it makes; in other words, on poems dominated by vehicle rather than tenor. But poems that aim for a prosier statement may also be given to their own kinds of obscurity, quite apart from any of the gaudier tricks of language. Edwin Arlington Robinson from the start wanted to use a prosier language than his contemporaries were using, and even at its highest pitch his language is far calmer than the language of Hopkins or Crane. Because of the rather old-fashioned manner, his poems might be thought to go about their business with a kind of bluff, if ironic or rueful, straightforwardness. Yet any reader with more than a casual acquaintance with his work will have encountered poems of his that are totally resistant to analysis and, incidentally, none the better for it. There is a kind of Robinson poem, however, that stands somewhere in between, neither simply straightforward nor impenetrable. "Eros Turannos" is one of these, and some consider it the best thing he ever wrote:

> She fears him, and will always ask
> What fated her to choose him;
> She meets in his engaging mask
> All reasons to refuse him;

But what she meets and what she fears
Are less than are the downward years,
Drawn slowly to the foamless weirs
    Of age, were she to lose him.

Between a blurred sagacity
    That once had power to sound him,
And Love, that will not let him be
    The Judas that she found him,
Her pride assuages her almost,
As if it were alone the cost.—
He sees that he will not be lost,
    And waits and looks around him.

A sense of ocean and old trees
    Envelops and allures him;
Tradition, touching all he sees,
    Beguiles and reassures him;
And all her doubts of what he says
Are dimmed with what she knows of days—
Till even prejudice delays
    And fades, and she secures him.

The falling leaf inaugurates
    The reign of her confusion;
The pounding wave reverberates
    The dirge of her illusion;
And home, where passion lived and died,
Becomes a place where she can hide,
While all the town and harbor side
    Vibrate with her seclusion.

We tell you, tapping on our brows,
    The story as it should be,—
As if the story of a house
    Were told, or ever could be;
We'll have no kindly veil between
Her visions and those we have seen,—
As if we guessed what hers have been,
    Or what they are or would be.

> Meanwhile we do no harm; for they
> > That with a god have striven,
> Not hearing much of what we say,
> > Take what the god has given;
> Though like waves breaking it may be,
> Or like a changed familiar tree,
> Or like a stairway to the sea
> > Where down the blind are driven.

There are things about this poem we will never know, just as there are things about it we seem to have known even before we started reading it. For one of its secrets is that it is based on a classic story situation, one we may think we understand better than in fact we do simply because we recognize it. A woman of good standing in a small town marries for love, but marries beneath her; the man betrays her in some fashion, probably sexual; and for reasons the townspeople think they can guess at, the wife, being at the mercy of the tyrannical god of love, sticks with the husband. In general shape and outline, the story, or at least the circumstances of the situation, may remind you a little of Henry James's *Washington Square,* or even of the Faulkner short story "A Rose for Emily," though the outcome is in both examples dramatically different. Robinson's story is far more restrained than Faulkner's, for instance, but also more ambiguous, more obscure; nor is it only because of the differences between prose and verse that this is so. For that matter, "Eros Turannos" is one of those poems that show Robinson's interest in narrative writing (twenty years earlier he had tried unsuccessfully to write prose sketches), and almost everyone who comments on this poem calls it "novelistic." Such compression as it has comes off because the prose details are, practically speaking, left out; they have been transformed into generality, an abstract or summary; the language, instead of being heated-up and rich, seems barely adequate to contain the force of the bottled-up emotion of the poem, which keeps threatening to break out. One might argue over whether or not, in the three particularized images with which the poem reaches its climax, it does finally break out. But even in this Robinsonian equivalent of a purple passage the language does not have the high-key intensity of Hopkins or Crane, and we need not put this down so much to the time and place of the poem—New England, early this century—or even to the temperament of the author, as to a clear esthetic choice.

Mildly Jamesian, the method involves a high degree of indirection in the telling of the tale, though with less willful withholding or post-poning of vital information than in many Robinson poems. His "En Passant," for example, is hopelessly lost to us because the information necessary to reconstruct the dramatic situation is refused us. Not so with "Eros Turannos": its obscurity is a good deal more subtle. It is tempting to feel that the moral complexity Robinson sees in the situation is responsible for the mild bewilderment we are left with, and I believe it is the method itself that allows one to think that. We learn, rather late in the poem, that the facts of the case—or what we must take to be the facts, since they are all we have—are being provided by the townspeople, a sort of civic chorus on the fringes of this small-town tragedy. It is their gossip we hear, and even they seem to have some doubts as to the reliability of their interpretation, as the next-to-last stanza attempts to explain.

So small a technical matter as the handling of the verb tenses contributes to the overall obscurity. In the last three stanzas we can be sure that we are lodged in the present, but before that we can hardly help wondering whether Robinson is dealing with some stage of the courtship or with the early days of the marriage, or even perhaps with the tragic present. The woman's fear of the loneliness of old age "were she to lose him"—does that come before their marriage or after? Is it a motive for marrying or a motive for staying married? As presented, it seems almost to be both; and that uncertainty, if it does rise to the level of consciousness, may serve the poem a little by adding to its sense of moral complexity, even though by way of a slight confusion. This is fairly shaky ground, I realize, but such ambiguities are best when felt to be rooted in the emotional complications of situation or statement, as they are here. And, indeed, compared to the obscurities that now, at the end of the "modern" century, are accepted as standard practice, with little or no attempt to rationalize them, Robinson's are hardly worth making much of a fuss over. But to persist: when she "secures him"—does this not sound as if she has just "caught" him, as a spinster catches an elusive bachelor? Yet it comes midway through the poem, and thus, if the poem had been developed in chronological order, it comes well along the time line of the action. And "secures" is as ambiguous as any word in the poem. It could mean also that she binds him to her with renewed force; or even that she provides him with the security of her house and goods, making him secure, as he evidently wishes to be. The meanings do not exactly conflict but, on first acquaintance with the rather bald and bleak style of the poem, the way they commingle and coexist comes as something of a surprise. Instead of the words' adding richness and resonance to the scene, as in the Hopkins poem, the dramatic situation here seems to add a suggestiveness and depth to the unspectacular words of the poem. It is as if we caught glimpses of a moral complexity through the chinks in the logic of its expression. If this is so, we can at least suggest that some of the obscurity is expressive of the very understanding the poem means to carry. Some of the obscurity is a reflection and by-product of Robinson's choice of the anonymous town gossips as tellers of the tale, since they can hardly be omniscient. (This is a familiar device in short stories, as in the Faulkner story already mentioned.) Due to the method, some of the deepest truths of character and situation are bound to remain hidden and uncertain; or the method is chosen in order to keep these truths dark. As the poet Robert Mezey puts it, Robinson doesn't like to tell you anything he doesn't know for sure, and that includes practically everything.

But it would be wrong in any case to push too far in any search for final truths here. That the woman's seclusion points to madness, as has been suggested, strikes me as farfetched, too much a novelistic cliché to have tempted Robinson; nor are we required to believe that she commits suicide (by drowning, presumably), though there is a fairly high suicide rate among Robinson's characters. The truth, whatever it may be, is held in suspension, unresolved: that itself is the resolution, the final truth. If the poem seems in the end somehow more definite than this as you look back on it, put it down to the eloquence of the last stanza and especially of the last three or four lines, which are bound to ring and echo in the memory as if no more could possibly have been said.

In neither the Robinson nor the Hopkins poem does the initial puzzlement or uncertainty entirely disappear; it seems instead to become embedded in one's experience of the poem and inextricable from it. To claim the uncertainty itself as part of the proper meaning would be to go too far, but it comes fairly near the truth, so near as to be worth being wrong about. In a poem like "Spelt from Sybil's Leaves" it is the language and the rhythm—aspects of the vehicle—that demand attention from the start, that never, for that matter, let go; what for convenience I have called the meaning depends on the language for its first life. In "Eros Turannos" the conditions are reversed. Here it is the meaning—which is to say the plot—that takes over; it is the tenor that dominates. The language probably needs to be capable of rising to a modestly excited level from time to time, as it does, but basically merely to be adequate will do.

There must be dozens of other types of obscurity, some driven by theory, some of course quite accidental, and whether any or all could seem as benign as the types we have been dealing with seems problematic. Both the Hopkins and the Robinson examples are strong enough by nature—by what, without reference to the meters and the rhyming, we ought to be willing to call form—to support a measure of obscurity without the integrity of the poem being seriously compromised. Indeed, in both poems the obscurity seems unavoidable; unless we could somehow see much more deeply into them, I do not believe we could ever say that the poems could have come into existence—could go on existing now—without it. And therefore the obscurity is no handicap, perhaps even has its uses. Can we claim this much?

Challenges More Than Solutions

Romulus Linney

I can offer you challenges more than solutions, since great plays are great mysteries and always will be.

Let me begin with two assumptions. One, you have already completed a first draft, and two, you believe that dramatic action is the key to revising a play.

Craft is not the priority in writing a first draft. What lies in your subconscious is that. What you care about deeply is that. Some kind of connection between your past, reaching far back into childhood and even infancy, crossing something that happened to you maybe yesterday, is that. Tennessee Williams, our host from the past at Sewanee, said somewhere that art lives in the subconscious, and he is right, along with Goethe, who said, "The will cannot do the work of the imagination."

My second assumption is that no matter how beautiful the language, how deep the conception, how subtle the irony, how exalted the philosophy, if you don't have a solid dramatic action to drive the play, it will not work.

So you've written a draft. It has a reading. It has fine things in it. Time goes by. You realize not everything in it was all that fine, and that something vital is missing. You must revise and search.

Let me suggest ten craft guidelines for revision of the play you have written.

One: Basic emotion. Audiences come to the theater seeking themselves. Plays reach their heights fueled not primarily by philosophy or politics or poetry but by the basic, familiar emotions of infancy, the powerful feelings we all experience during the first year of life and know well. Fear, rage, desire, sorrow, glee, envy, jealousy, love, hate, and so on. Othello, Lear, Oedipus, Hamlet, as well as Willy Loman, Beckett's tramps, and David Mamet's salesmen are alive with these emotions, with variations and combinations of them, seemingly adult but actually infantile, as we discover when Othello kills his wife in rage and Oedipus tears out his own eyes.

Two: Dramatic event. This is not a lyrical, narrative, psychological, or symbolic event, but the actual happening during the action. Ball game, bullfight, car wreck, more than poetry reading. Playwrights too subtle put their audiences to sleep, which can be a brutal awakening for the playwright. Opportunistic playwrights too quick to be bold can be silly, and lose their audiences laughing after intermission. Something in between is necessary, and that is an adult, understandable dramatic action that the audience realizes is about them. They must see themselves in no uncertain terms. Any good play that you have seen, the minute you speak its name, jumps complete into your mind. Again, Othello, Oedipus, and company: their actions are so strong, simple, consistent, and universal that you don't have to say anything else to know exactly where you are. So how can I simplify my dramatic event, strengthen it, make it plain, like keeping Mama off dope in *Long Day's Journey Into Night*.

Three: Conflict and stakes of conflict. Not as crude as blowing up the White House but not as subtle as changing somebody's mind about civilization. Obvious conflict is not banal or obvious when a production is at stake, and actors want to know what they are doing onstage. This may seem simplistic but it is vital. Hamlet perishes, and with him perish great qualities that would have ruled Denmark. There is conflict with a renegade king and conflict with himself as this wonderful young man tries to do something his better self cries out against: revenge but also murder. Music may be about joy and poetry about perception; drama is about people fighting with each other in some way. It is about coming to terms with life as it is, a good definition of any play by critic Kenneth Tynan.

Four: Action and progression of action. Begin something and watch it develop. Don't beat it to death; move it along, let it reverse itself, contain surprises and discoveries. Every scene must contain something not in the scene before it, and this should be a surprise, a discovery. Read Dürrenmatt's *The Visit* as a perfect example.

Five: Dialogue. How people talk in your play depends on a dance of two things: lifelikeness—that is, people speaking, even in verse or a foreign accent, in a believable way—and how they move the action along. Hard to put together. Arthur Wing Pinero wrote superbly accurate dialogue, much more true to life than George Bernard Shaw's, but Shaw's dialogue moves us swiftly through changing situations, keeping everything alive. Skill in human speech is only one aspect of dialogue. An exercise. Tape-record people talking at a party or a restaurant, without their knowledge. Be careful, but do it. Listen to it. People do amazing things talking: they interrupt each other, jump ahead when they see the point is taken, follow no grammar, delight in duels, use all kinds of spontaneous inventions, and so on. But if you put that onstage, after five minutes we sleep. Under the spontaneous and believable dialogue, the action must never stop developing. The two dancing together delight us. Balance these elements carefully.

Six: Group mind. This is a phrase of Thornton Wilder's and it is crucial. The mind and emotions of an audience concentrate very slowly at first. You need to let the audience see that the actors are people like them, in some place they can accept. You unify them with a subject vital to them. After that, an audience transforms itself. It becomes lightning fast. If you dwell and repeat then, the group mind gets impatient with you because it is ahead of you. Be slow and true to reality with your audience at first; then trust it to know more than you do later on. A thousand people erupting into a huge laugh in one instant at Molière is what I mean, as well as that deep silence in the presence of Oedipus when Sophocles has him discover who he is.

Seven: Main character. The most common cause of a fuzzy play is uncertainty of the character it is about. My friend Marsha Norman says this very well: every play is about one person. Everyone else is secondary, even when they are most often onstage. In structure, *Long Day's Journey into Night* is about the mother, because she makes everything happen. Everything her husband and sons do and say in this great play is about what has happened to them after she took dope—iron unification that allows a lot of wonderful speeches on other aspects of their common family life. Chekhov's *The Wood Demon* is a lovable and funny but impossible play, with a murder and a suicide back to back at the end. Compare it with *Uncle Vanya*, a masterpiece and a great example of revision, since Chekhov rewrote *The Wood Demon* into *Uncle Vanya*. The main revision was to center the action on Vanya instead of the Dr. Astrov character, on whom it was centered in *The Wood Demon*. The doctor is still a great creation but one in better focus with Vanya as the main character.

Eight: Blood relationships, counting lovers. Few plays are about anything else, since it is hard to unify the fifty to one thousand people in the audience with other subjects. We want to know about our families, including lovers, who are families to be. *Faust, Macbeth, Life with Father, Who's Afraid of Virginia Woolf*? But *Julius Caesar*—What blood relations there? Well, Caesar is a father figure, murdered by sort of rebellious sons and avenged by an Antony who looked to him as a father.

Nine: Reversals and obstacles. These are technical means that can accomplish great things. Reversals in a play, where things turn out to be the opposite of what was expected, mirror one of the great conditions of life. Things don't work out the way we thought they would: careers, marriages, children, hopes, and dreams: who can say they do? When plays reflect this, audiences recognize their truth. When they don't, audiences know better. Of total reversals in plays Shaw was the master, making this one technical device his basic strategy. Read "Don Juan in Hell" from *Man and Superman*. Everything is turned upside down, effectively and truthfully.

Ten: Lifting a play. This is my term for that theatrical invention, often from production colleagues, that gives the action of the play a "lift" that takes it into much greater realms of intensity. It should be searched after by every playwright for every play, because it can make all the difference. Fine acting is of course the first to be desired. One great modern example. Seeing the Lunts act *The Visit* is very different from seeing it performed by good but not great actors. Another example are the horses in Peter Shaffer's *Equus*. Putting metal sculptured frames of horses' heads on several big men and putting them on built-up boots created the horse on stage in that play. So when the disturbed boy rode on one of them naked at night, masturbating, Peter Firth could climb onto a man's back, and the audience accepted him as riding a horse naked, yelling when he ejaculated. This electrifying moment could occur in front of us, rather than just be described. Laurence Olivier, in his famous *Oedipus,* imitated baby seals in Alaska, who in spring, trying to eat grass, get their tongues frozen to the ice and emit horrifying screams, recordings of which gave Olivier the blood-freezing cry of his Oedipus with his eyes torn out. The idea of bringing onstage a strange wooden horse for Frederick the Great to ride helped a play of mine not only be more exciting but get written at all. Hamlet's father as a real ghost instead of some letters or gossip, the sane/mad asylum of *Marat/Sade*—these are examples of devices that lift a play into theatrical intensity and dramatic beauty.

I offer a very modest example, and such as it is, an eight-minute play of my own that does, I believe, contain some aspect of each of these ten notions.

CLAIR DE LUNE

[*Moonlight. Enter* ABEL, *carrying two beers, a small wooden box, and an aluminum-plastic beach chair.*]

Abel: Come on out, Mother! If I have to hear it again I want to listen to it out here! [*Enter* LUCILLE, *with a second chair and a small tape recorder with a cassette in it. She is looking at the cassette case.*]

Lucille: All right, Father. I'll play it in the moonlight! [*She puts down her chair, sits in it, places the tape recorder on the box.*]

Abel: Here's your beer, Mother. Let 'er rip! [*Lucille takes the beer, plays the cassette. On the little recorder, an orchestra plays "Clair de Lune." They listen.* LUCILLE *sighs.*]

Lucille: That's so pretty. Classics of the Night, it says here. That little piece means Moonlight, it says here. Who'd ever think a body could get so much pleasure out of one little tune. [*Abel takes a fishing reel out of his pocket.*]

Abel: Mother, I hope you do. You play it enough. [*It gets suddenly darker.*] Whup. There goes your moon, Mother. Right behind a cloud.

Lucille: Oh, fish. It was so pretty, a-shining on the lake. Like the music.

Abel: Thought we'd get a look at the camp swans. Beautiful critters, swans in the moonlight. Mean, though! All took up with theirselves. Hiss at ye! Peck ye! Can't tolerate nobody else but theirselves.

Lucille: Swans in the moonlight. The pleasures of Florida.

Abel: Yep. Beer! Trailer! Swans!

Lucille: Retirement, Father.

Abel: That's it, Mother! Retirement! [*He looks at his reel. "Clair de Lune" plays.*]

Lucille: Father?

Abel: Yes, Mother?

Lucille: We do right, coming here?

Abel: I think we did.

Lucille: We could have farmed another two years, maybe more.

Abel: But we didn't.

Lucille: I know we didn't, and I know I said yes, all right, let's go, but now, I just don't know.

Abel: Don't know what, Mother?

Lucille: If we should have come here. [*The segment of "Clair de Lune" ends, fading away suddenly, replaced by a Strauss waltz. She turns off the recorder, rewinds the cassette.*] I just don't know.

Abel: Yes, you do. You know what's wrong. Say it.

Lucille: I miss my children!

Abel: [*Quietly.*] Do you?

Lucille: Yes! [*Pause.*] I do!

Abel: Uh-huh.

Lucille: But it is peaceful here. I do like that.

Abel: So do I. No more phone calls in the middle of the night. Yelling and sobbing and screaming and crying. Weddings, divorces, other man's wife, other woman's man, whiskey, dope, and God knows what else. Pistols twice, shotgun once. Fists through windows, bloody shirts and dresses torn apart, abortions and carwrecks. Carwrecks! Eight of them, eight! Count 'em! Eight carwrecks! God Almighty!

Lucille: We got in trouble.

Abel: THEY got in trouble. Four trips to hell in a county courthouse. Half the crop going every other year to a goddamned lawyer. All the world shaking its head at our children we done our best to bring up right! Mother! Let them untangle their own lives, and leave us to find a little peace in ours!

Lucille: But why? That's what I keep wondering about. Our children! Why!

Abel: We don't know why! Neither does nobody else, judges, police, doctors, nobody! Children go crazy. We done our best by 'em, left 'em half the farm, now to hell with it! We have earned our rest!

Lucille: We gave them half the farm but was that enough? What I keep thinking about, Father, is what we didn't give them. Couldn't give them.

Abel: What's that?

Lucille: Joy! Some real pleasure in life! You know. What we had together. What we always had together!

Abel: Mother, I don't think anybody can give anybody that!

Lucille: But why not! They ought to! I tried to tell Sarah once, what it was like, seeing you for the first time, and not liking you at all, and then you just waiting for me, and waiting for me—

Abel: Well, I knew, Mother. I just knew!

Lucille: And from the first time, everything, I mean the first TIME together, like that, well now! Well now!

Abel: Mother—

Lucille: I mean!

Abel: Mother!

Lucille: I mean!

Abel: Mother, stop fretting about this!

Lucille: But it was good! It was always good! God help us, Father, after all these years, it's good now!

Abel: I know that!

Lucille: Then why not for them? Not one, not ONE of them! What is it we have, just took for granted, they can't never find, no matter how hard they try?

Abel: Now Mother, hush up!

Lucille: I WILL NOT! I never in my life wanted no man but you! And if what you're always telling me is the truth—

Abel: Truth, Mother! Only time I tried anybody else, I got sick, you know that!

Lucille: Then why? WHY? What did we have all them years, working and sweating and farming and making do, they couldn't have too? WHAT DID WE DO WRONG?

Abel: NOTHING! THEY did all that! Hush up!!

Lucille: WHAT DID GOD GIVE US HE KEPT FROM THEM?? *[It suddenly gets brighter.]*

Abel: Look, Mother. There's your moon again. Play that tune for yourself, and settle down. I don't want to hear this no more.

Lucille: All right. *[She plays "Clair de Lune" again. Pause.]*

Abel: There! Look, by God! *[They both point, staring at the lake.]*

Lucille: Swans, Father!

Abel: Swans! In the moonlight! *[Pause. Slowly.]* Strange looking critters. Jest gliding along.

Lucille: I don't think I like them so much.

Abel: Cause they're mean. Look good, but they're cold and mean inside. All took up with theirselves. Come between two swans, you get pecked to death!

Lucille: Who'd want to come between them?

Abel: I don't know. Somebody.

Lucille: "The swan is a beauty easy to take,
          Two are better, upon the lake."

Abel: You just make that up?

Lucille: No. Read it, yesterday.

Abel: Where?

Lucille: Reader's Digest.

Abel: Oh.

Lucille: It was in some article about zoos. [*Pause. She turns off the music.*] I miss my children. [*Pause.*]

Abel: Yeah. [*He spins his reel. The moonlight fades.*]

Bend Sinister: A Handbook for Writers

Alice McDermott

I am wary of any advice to fiction writers that smacks of "how to."

I am happy to see fiction writers gainfully employed and serially published, but I am always hit with a wave of disappointment when a fiction writer I admire brings forth a book or an article about writing fiction.

I have never been a student in a writing workshop where the phrases "a short story must never" or "a novel must always" didn't fill me with the determination to write a story that did what it mustn't or a novel that didn't do what it must.

And in the twenty years I've been leading writing workshops I have never answered any question that begins, "Are you allowed to . . ." or ends, "Can you do that?" with anything more precise than "You can do whatever you can get away with."

In a recent workshop at Sewanee, Ernest Gaines said—I think it was on the very first day—"No one can tell you how to write your stories. They're your stories. You have to write what you have to write your way. No one can tell you how." He said it so reasonably, and dismissively, that

I could immediately see heads nodding all around the room, one whispered "Of course" being exchanged with another. And then, a split second later, across those same nodding faces, there passed a shadow of utter dismay—a series, one after the other, of shifty-eyed glances. "Then what the hell are we doing here?" was the unmurmured murmur that filled the room. "What the hell are we paying for?"

As much as we may eschew them, we all want "how tos." Instruction manuals, guidebooks, handbooks. We want some help writing these stories that are indeed our stories that no one can tell us how to write. I have written four novels thus far, and each one of them, in the midst of its composition, has felt to me like groping in the dark, going down blind alleys, building castles in the sand at 3 A.M.—choose what cliché you will, but make sure it is a cliché that refers to darkness, uncertainty, and a numbing sense of utter futility. For the first half of the composition of each of my novels I have been consumed by a sense of not knowing what I'm doing, and for the second half I have been consumed by the certainty that I know exactly what I am doing and should not be doing it.

I have at these times longed for handbooks myself—something I could pluck off a shelf, check the index, find my particular problem (characters are boring, plot is missing, author is questioning the meaning of her existence), refer to the proper pages, read, nod, and then return to the writing with the solution in hand.

No such handbook exists, of course, and if it did I wouldn't waste my time reading it or taking its advice, since such handbooks must, by their very nature, be as general and precise as a horoscope, and since I am a fiction writer and harbor in my heart—as we all do—the conviction that no one can tell me how to write my stories because no one who has lived my life and thought my thoughts has ever written this story before.

(I've noticed, as a matter of fact, in my years of teaching, that one of the most subtly disconcerting things a writer can say to a student goes something like this, "John Cheever [or Updike or Chekhov or Flannery O'Connor, or Munro or James or whoever] did exactly what you're attempting here in a story called. . . ." That slow burn you can detect behind the student's enthusiastic nod as she diligently copies down a title is, I believe, the one true indication of a real writer, a real writer who even as she obediently copies down the suggested reading is thinking, *No one has ever done exactly what I'm attempting to do here, you stupid ass.*)

No one can tell us how to write our stories. But I do find that we can be shored up at those dark moments during the composition of a work of fiction by taking from a shelf a great novel or short story and reading again something that made us want to get into this racket in the first place (because we're all readers first, and we all become writers because we have been inspired to try our own hand by something we have read). I find, too, that I can illustrate, if not illuminate, my advice to other writers that in fiction you can do whatever you can get away with by directing them toward novels and stories that do just that. Nabokov's *Bend Sinister* is quite often, for me, one of the first novels to come to mind.

I will not presume to lecture you on the merits of Nabokov's novel. I will not pretend to understand or even to appreciate fully all of its wordplay and allusion and cross-language sleight of hand. The foreword Nabokov wrote for the novel in 1963, contained in the Vintage edition that seems to be available everywhere, is quite enough to set you agape at his brilliance even before you've read the first page, and I must confess that I seem to be one of the readers he refers to in that foreword when he says, "Most people will not even mind having missed all this" (that is, the cross references, the wordplay, the hidden codes and themes); "well-wishers will bring their own symbols and mobiles and portable radios to my little party."

What I bring to each reading of this wonderful novel (besides my humble hat in my hand and my delight to encounter once again each delicious morsel) is my conviction that if ever there was one, this is a handbook for writers.

And at the risk of oversimplifying a complex and indescribable work of art, it is as a handbook for writers that I'd like to refer to *Bend Sinister* today.

❧

I'll begin, as most handbooks do, with "Beginnings" or, for the less stouthearted, the more gentle "Getting Started" or, if our handbook is to appeal to the more commercially minded writer: "Drawing Your Reader In on the First Page" (which might be followed by the warning that the world is full of distractions and if you don't catch your reader's attention with the first page, you may never catch it at all!).

Here is how Nabokov begins his novel:

> An oblong puddle inset in the coarse asphalt; like a fancy footprint filled to the brim with quicksilver; like a spatulate hole through which you can see the nether sky. Surrounded. I note, by a diffuse tentacled black dampness where

some dull dun dead leaves have stuck. Drowned, I should say, before the puddle had shrunk to its present size.

(A first sentence made up of three phrases joined by semicolons, followed by a single-word sentence, "Surrounded." Blatant alliteration, second person, and first person in a novel that is to be predominately third person, a detailed description of a puddle—can you do that?)

It lies in shadow but contains a sample of the brightness beyond, where there are trees and two houses. Look closer. Yes, it reflects a portion of pale blue sky—mild infantile shade of blue—taste of milk in my mouth because I had a mug of that colour thirty-five years ago. It also reflects a brief tangle of bare twigs and the brown sinus of a stouter limb cut off by its rim and a transverse bright cream-coloured band. You have dropped something, this is yours, creamy house in the sunshine beyond.

When the November wind has its recurrent icy spasms, a rudimentary vortex of ripples creases the brightness of the puddle.

(Are you allowed to have the whole first page of the novel go by without any indication of who, what, when, where, or why we should keep reading?)

Two leaves, two triskelions, like two shuddering three-legged bathers coming at a run for a swim, are borne by their impetus right into the middle where with a sudden slowdown they float quite flat. Twenty minutes past four.

View from a hospital window.

November trees, poplars, I imagine, two of them growing straight out of the asphalt: all of them in the cold bright sun, bright richly furrowed bark and an intricate sweep of numberless burnished bare twigs, old gold—because getting more of the falsely mellow sun in the higher air. Their immobility is in contrast with the spasmodic ruffling of the inset reflection—for the visible emotion of a tree is in the mass of its leaves, and there remain hardly more than thirty-seven or so here and there on one side of the tree. They just flicker a little, of a neutral tint, but burnished by the sun to the same ikontinct as the intricate trillions of twigs. Swooning blue of the sky crossed by pale motionless superimposed cloud wisps.

The operation has not been successful and my wife will die.

Who could formulate the advice that would produce such a beginning? The writer takes you by the scruff of the neck and, first and foremost, makes you see. A world forms before your eyes even before you know what or who the novel is about, a world of color and light and shape and voice—"taste of milk in my mouth. . . . You have dropped something, this is yours . . . poplars, I imagine"—voice that insinuates itself so subtly into the description that we are hardly aware of it, hardly aware of the way it transforms a scene being observed into a scene being observed *by someone* until the devastating single line "The operation has not been successful and my wife will die" appears (bringing with it, by the way, plot, story) and we can sense, if we can't quite see, how those first person references have set us up to receive its full impact.

This "I," this stranger, this creature wholly unknown to us four paragraphs ago when we first opened this oddly-titled novel by some Russian guy whose name nobody can seem to agree about how to pronounce, this "I" became human for us when we tasted, with him, tasted the memory of that milk in the blue cup of his childhood and observed, with him, the details of his reflections, the reflection in the puddle seen from the hospital window where the operation was not successful and his wife will die.

> Beyond a low fence, in the sun, in the bright starkness, a slaty house front has for frame two cream-coloured lateral pilasters and a broad blank unthinking cornice: the frosting of a shopworn cake. Windows look black by day. Thirteen of them; white lattice, green shutters. All very clear, but the day will not last. Something has moved in the blackness of one window: an ageless housewife—ope as my dentist in my milktooth days used to say, a Dr. Wollison—opens the window, shakes out something and you may now close.

The advice to writers, of course, is to take your reader by the scruff of the neck and make him see the world you are calling forth, remember the appeal of language used well and the necessity of voice, of the human, in the simplest descriptions and remember, too, that this is fiction you are writing, where every detail is chosen and every word purposeful and a necessary part not only of the sentence it is contained in but of the entire work as well.

The puddle here, for example, is not merely a narrative snapshot, a random subject upon which the talented artist/author can self-indulgently lavish minute details like so many swirls of paint, but a thematic tool as well.

Here is how the author refers to it in his prologue:

The plot starts to breed in the bright broth of a rain puddle.... The oblong pool, shaped like a cell that is about to divide, reappears subthematically throughout the novel, as an ink blot in Chapter Four, an inkstain in Chapter Five, spilled milk in Chapter Eleven, the infusoria-like image of ciliated thought in Chapter Twelve, the footprint of a phosphorescent islander in Chapter Eighteen, and the imprint a soul leaves in the intimate texture of space in the closing paragraph. The puddle thus kindled and rekindled in Krug's mind remains linked up with the image of his wife not only because he had contemplated the inset sunset from her death-bedside, but also because this little puddle vaguely evokes in him my link with him: a rent in his world leading to another world of tenderness, brightness and beauty.

The puddle, the novel's first image, resounds too in the choice of the title, which Nabokov further points out is a term from heraldry, a bar or band drawn from the left side, a title meant, he writes, "to suggest an outline broken by refraction, a distortion in the mirror of being, a wrong turn taken by life, a sinistral and sinister world."

Advice to writers: know what you've written and why it belongs in a work of art, where what actually exists and what really happens or has happened is mostly irrelevant, where how each detail is a part of the whole is all that really counts.

Helpful hint: you do not need to know this before you begin to compose, or even while you compose; you should aspire only to know it when you have brought your work to a close and have had a chance, yourself, to grasp the meaning of your work, in its entirety.

Borges said that "good readers are poets as singular, and as awesome, as great authors themselves," and he called reading "an activity subsequent to writing—more resigned, more civil, more intellectual." It seems to me that in the course of the composition of any work of fiction there comes a time when the writer must become a reader. This time may occur after the white head of inspiration (or, for those of us who hesitate to apply such words as *inspiration,* the white heat—or maybe just the glowing embers, steadily puffed upon—of simply getting down a first or second draft); it may be—more likely—interspersed between a number of such moments—but whenever it occurs, it is that necessary time when the writer sits back (breathless, no doubt, wiping a brow) and the calm (more resigned, more civil, more intellectual) reader in the writer takes over. It is this calm reader who must ultimately make sure that in the over-

whelming rush inspired words are correctly chosen and fully meaningful and that the piece of fiction works as a whole.

Chapter Two of our handbook might be headed: "Character." Or, for
the egomaniac mad scientist in all of us who write fiction, "Bringing
People to Life."

Once again, Nabokov first and foremost makes you see. You can haul
out E. M. Forster's labels for flat characters and round characters, you can
distinguish major from minor, bit players from stars, but, let's face it,
when you are caught in the spell of a work, when you are a reader absorbed, you only notice there or not there. Nabokov characters are there.

The housekeeper in Krug's apartment—a bit player, to be sure, meant
only to look after his eight-year-old son while Krug is staring out of a
hospital window, negotiating the mad crossing of a bridge guarded by
the imbecilic soldiers of his country's new imbecilic police state, and returning home a widower—is blessed with full life in these two sentences:
"She had been in the family for several years and, as conventionally happens in such cases, was pleasantly plump, middle-aged, and sensitive.
There she stood staring at him with dark liquid eyes, her mouth slightly
opened showing a gold spotted tooth, her coral earrings staring too and
one hand pressed to her formless grey-worsted bosom."

I love the economy of this description; background is there, as is the
acknowledgment of the character as a type ("as conventionally happens in
such cases"). Only her eyes and mouth and bosom are mentioned, but
nevertheless we see her perfectly—and those staring coral earrings that
manage to convey a sense of her life thus far (before she makes her brief
appearance in the novel) as well as her present fear and heartache and as-
tonishment.

And here is another character coming to life, old Professor Azureus
from the same university where Krug is a famous philosopher. It is a description without the precise physical detail of eye color or earring, and
yet it is as vivid and revealing of character as any I've read:

Old Azureus's manner of welcoming people was a silent rhapsody. Ecstat-
ically beaming, slowly, tenderly, he would take your hand between his soft
palms, hold it thus as if it were a long sought treasure or a sparrow all fluff
and heart, in moist silence, peering at you the while with his beaming wrinkles
rather than with his eyes, and then, very slowly, the silvery smile would start to
dissolve, the tender old hands would gradually release their hold, a blank

expression replace the fervent light of his pale fragile face, and he would leave you as if he had made a mistake, as if after all you were not the loved one—the loved one whom, the next moment, he would espy in another corner, and again the smile would dawn, again the hands would enfold the sparrow, again it would all dissolve.

Eye color, hair color, the color of his pants or his vest—none of this needs to be told about old Azureus because in this one paragraph the reader has met the man and taken his measure. And the beaming wrinkles, the pale fragile face are not merely parts of a catalog of physical features that another, earnest author might relate in order to make a body vivid—they are the physical details that reveal the character of the man, even as they make us see.

Nabokov's brilliant physical description of Adam Krug in the same chapter is a guide to exactly what is required of the fiction writer in order to bring characters to life, a kind of metaphor for the depth of awareness the writer must have in order to make his characters live:

> He was a big heavy man in his early forties, with untidy, dusty, or faintly grizzled locks and a roughly hewn face suggestive of the uncouth chess master or of the morose composer, but more intelligent. The strong compact dusky forehead had that peculiar hermetic aspect (a bank safe? a prison wall?) which the brows of thinkers possess. The brain consisted of water, various chemical compounds and a group of highly specialized fats. The pale steely eyes were half closed in their squarish orbits under the shaggy eyebrows. . . . The ears were of goodly size with hair inside. . . . He wore a badly creased dark suit and a bow tie. . . . The not so recent collar was of the low open variety, i.e. with a comfortable triangular space for his namesake's apple. Thick-soled shoes and old-fashioned black spats were the distinctive characters of his feet. What else? Oh, yes—the absent minded beat of his forefinger against the arm of his chair.
>
> Under this visible surface, a silk shirt enveloped his robust torso and tired hips. It was tucked deep into his long underpants which in their turn were tucked into his socks; it was rumoured, he knew, that he wore none (hence the spats) but that was not true; they were in fact nice expensive lavender silk socks.
>
> Under this was the warm white skin. Out of the dark an ant trail, a narrow capillary caravan, went up the middle of his abdomen to end at the brink of his navel; and a blacker and denser growth was spread-eagled upon his chest.
>
> Under this was a dead wife and a sleeping child.

A catalog of physical attributes, of course, but the master novelist understands, too, what is at the center—the soul, the heart of each player, minor or major, flat or round—and subtly, carefully, in every description he writes, reveals all.

I'd like to title another chapter in this handbook for writers: "You Can Do Whatever You Can Get Away With." You've already seen—I hope—that kind of audacity in the first paragraphs of *Bend Sinister,* but let me just cite another example (the novel is full of them) that would never pass muster in any number of writing workshops: the unwarranted person or point-of-view shift. (Those of us who are paid to do such things generally write "p. of v." in the margins of your unrepeatable, unprecedented, irreplaceable stories when this occurs.) Here is Krug calling his friend Ember on the night of Olga's death:

> Ember might be out. The telephone might not work. But from the feel of the receiver as he took it up he knew the faithful instrument was alive. I could never remember Ember's number. Here is the back of the telephone book on which we used to jot down names and figures, our hands mixed, slanting and curving in opposite directions. Her concavity fitting my convexity exactly. Extraordinary—I am able to make out the shadow of eyelashes on the child's cheek but fail to decipher my own handwriting. He found his spare glasses and then the familiar number with the six in the middle resembling Ember's Persian nose, and Ember put down his pen, removed the long amber cigarette-holder from his thickly pursed lip and listened.
>
> "I was in the middle of this letter when Krug rang up and told me a terrible thing. Poor Olga is no more."

An unlawful shift of both point of view and person, as well as a non-transitioned total change of scene, that saves both reader and author from the pathos of the actual phone conversation and allows Ember the chance to recollect and thus reveal the history of his friendship with Krug, so smoothly executed that only those of us who read with red pencils in hand will know it even happened.

Further examples, as I said, abound: the manipulative use of dreams to give background and develop character. Long, delightful but didactic passages that however briefly put the story on hold to explore the nature of thought, God, Shakespeare, school yard bullies, the futility of translation.

A chapter that begins: "'We met yesterday,' said the room. 'I am the spare bedroom in the Maximovs' dacha. These are windmills on the wallpaper.' 'That's right,' replied Krug."

A final blatant, authorial intrusion that should prove E. M. Forster's claim that all such intrusions decrease the "emotional temperature" of the piece but that manages, nevertheless, to do quite the opposite, leaving the reader (leaving this reader) still quite warm, thank you, fully involved, amazed at how that initial rent in the world, the little puddle glimpsed from the hospital window, has given way to another place, "of tenderness, lightness and beauty"—the room in which the author writes.

We'll need a chapter on detail—not that the use of detail hasn't already been mentioned, and not so our handbook can belabor the obvious, *i.e.*, detail is good, precise detail is better, precise detail with many layers of meaning that contributes to the harmony and shape of the whole work is better still—but so we can understand the meaning of detail as used by fiction writers.

Here is Krug, crossing the bridge on his way home from the hospital:

> Presently he stopped again. Let us touch this and look at this. In the faint light (of the moon? of his tears? of the few lamps the dying fathers of the city had lit from a mechanical sense of duty?) his hand found a certain pattern of roughness: a furrow in the stone of the parapet and a knob and a hole with some moisture inside—all of it highly magnified as the 30,000 pits in the crust of the plastic moon are on the large glossy print which the proud selenographer shows his young wife. On this particular night, just after they had tried to turn over to me her purse, her comb, her cigarette holder, I found and touched this—a selected combination, details of the bas-relief. I had never touched this particular knob before and shall never find it again. This moment of conscious contact holds a drop of solace. The emergency brake of time. Whatever the present moment is, I have stopped it. Too late. In the course of our, let me see, twelve, twelve and three months, years of life together, I ought to have immobilized by this simple method millions of moments; paying perhaps terrific fines, but stopping the train. Say, why did you do it? the popeyed conductor might ask. Because I liked the view. Because I wanted to stop those speeding trees and the path twisting between them. By stepping on its receding tail. What happened to her would perhaps not have happened, had I been in the habit of stopping this or that bit of our common life, prophylactically, prophetically, letting this or that moment rest and breathe in peace. Taming time. Giving her pulse respite. Pampering life, life—our patient.

That's why we use detail, to tame time, to step on life's receding tail. We use precise detail in fiction not merely because it makes for better, more vivid writing; we use detail because the moment of conscious contact holds a drop of solace.

And then there's plot. Yes, sooner or later our handbook will have to have a chapter about plot.

The easiest piece of advice to follow in regard to plot might be to proclaim yourself a literary writer, the author of "serious literature"—which our author refers to in his foreword as "a euphemism for the hollow profundity and the ever-welcome commonplace"—and declare plot irrelevant, bourgeois, false, unnecessary, regressive, whatever, and then dispense with it entirely—leaving your readers and your colleagues to wonder if your disdain is authentic or only a response to your discovery that developing plot is so damn hard.

I've been trying to avoid, you may have noticed, telling you too much about the novel as a whole, because I would really love for you all to read it yourselves, and there's nothing worse than bringing someone else's lame description of a story to your own first reading. (You know that any book review in which the reviewer says, "I won't be giving too much away by saying . . ." usually does.) In fact, I think my own initial thrill at discovering the work of Vladimir Nabokov can be attributed to my never having heard anything about his work before. Thanks to my less-than-rigorous, rather spotty education in literature, I first took a book of his short stories from the local library only because I had a vague idea that I had seen his name before—I may actually have been thinking of Turgenev—and once I began to read them I felt I was a regular Columbus, my delight in the prose almost matched by the self-satisfaction I felt in having rescued this poor unknown, exiled-in-Switzerland, and clearly disappointed old writer from total oblivion.

But there is a good deal to be learned about plot in *Bend Sinister,* and so for the briefest and vaguest plot summary available, I'll go to the Vintage edition again, not to the author's foreword but to the editor's jacket copy: "A haunting and compelling narrative about a civilized man and his child caught up in the tyranny of a police state. Professor Adam Krug, the country's foremost philosopher, offers the only hope of resistance to Paduk, dictator and leader of the Party of the Average Man. In a folly of bureaucratic bungling and ineptitude, the government attempts to co-opt Krug's support in order to validate the new regime."

If this sounds very little like the novel I've been quoting from all along, then the first and foremost lesson in plot offered by *Bend Sinister* is coming clear. Without the particulars of Nabokov's language and wit and intelligence, the bare outline of the novel's plot seems rather bare indeed, certainly familiar enough, something like a number of other works that have dealt with the behind-the-iron-curtain/through-the-looking-glass madness from Solzhenitsyn to Kundera to Koestler and on across any number of political thrillers and propaganda tracts. It may even sound, from our vantage, a little dated. (The novel, after all, was published in 1947—helped along to its publication by Allen Tate, by the way.) Clichéd, even, in summary, what with the dictator Paduk being a petty beast, a former schoolmate of Krug who was, in the author's words, "regularly tormented by the boys, regularly caressed by the school janitor," a bitter and tyrannical child, a darling of the disenfranchised, suddenly made ultimate ruler, with the predictable results: mad bureaucratic entanglements, the sudden disappearance of even the most benign characters, the sudden transformation of others—deadly tantrums at the top.

And while it is easy enough to say that it is Nabokov's language and wit and intelligence that make the novel unique and raise it from familiar and commercial fiction to "serious literature," there is an aspect of the plot—an aspect not cited in the dust jacket description—that in reality (or in my opinion, whichever comes first) accounts for the novel's importance, and brilliance.

Nabokov himself says, "The story in *Bend Sinister* is not really about life and death in a grotesque police state. My characters are not 'types' or carriers of this or that 'idea.' . . . The main theme of *Bend Sinister* . . . is the beating of Krug's loving heart, the torture an intense tenderness is subjected to."

We've been shown that heart, quite literally, in the physical description of Krug, but it is not the presence of a beating heart in any given character that makes the difference; it is the fact that this heart is at the very center of the story itself, that it shapes the story, determines the plot, remains the novel's primary reason for being. The plot moves, turns, develops, not in order to accommodate the author's *cleverness* (and there is much cleverness in contemporary fiction), but to reveal, to record, the beating of Krug's loving heart.

Without that beating heart that shapes the story, the language, the wit, the allusions, the wordplay are reduced to mere moments of highly intelligent cleverness—delightful, yes, amusing, entertaining, funny (you have to read Krug's interview with Paduk), brilliant—but subject, finally, to the vicissitudes of time and politics and taste. Touching, finally, on nothing that—to use Faulkner's word—endures. It is the beating of Krug's loving heart that makes *Bend Sinister* great.

Advice to writers then: without that heart at the center of your fiction, advice can't help you. If it is there, then no one can—or needs to—tell you how to write your stories.

Highlights

Marsha Norman

I will admit being a little daunted by the prospects of giving a craft lecture to this group. What could I possibly know that you would find valuable? Writing plays and musicals and movies feels like a real low-down life most of the time, though truly, I wouldn't trade it. Actually, in one of my lowest career moments—you know: no jobs, no prospects, no ideas for jobs, no prospect of ideas—I had the startling revelation that this was the life where I got to be a writer, which is what I always wanted to be, that this life was the one I longed for in all the others. We have our ups and downs, our bad years and good, but we are a scrappy bunch, playwrights, and can be counted on to dance at parties and be loyal, but not always on time. So maybe we know something. Like how to survive. But are you really interested in plays, I wondered?

But then I remembered this odd idea you sometimes hear out there in the world, and that is that everybody has at least one play in them. And there does seem to be evidence for this: All the time people come up to me and say, Marsha, I have this great idea for a play. What they hope, of course, is that I will write their idea for them and make it as brilliant as they would if they only had the time to sit down and get the thing on paper. But alas, I tell them. The only person who can write your play is you. So on the off chance that you might be harboring the secret desire to write a play, I thought I'd just hit the highlights—what a play is, what a play has to do, and what mistakes you don't have to make if you ever sit down to write yours.

For starters, on the simplest possible level, a play is a piece of machinery. Like a ski lift. Like an automobile. Like an airplane. All of which may be beautiful in themselves, but which have a single justifying purpose, and that is to take you somewhere. In the case of a play, it must take you from where you are when you enter the theater to where you are when you leave. A play that doesn't take you someplace doesn't work. Instinctively, you know this. It doesn't move you, you say. You walk out and you say, "It didn't go anywhere," and you call up your friends and you tell them you hated it and they stay away and the show closes. Finally, the show moves, but it isn't to that great destination the playwright was hoping for.

As simple as this rule is, I cannot state it strongly enough. A play goes forward or dies. You can have the most fantastic Mercedes coupe in your driveway, and the finish can be flawless, and the seats can really be comfortable, and you can even have Harrison Ford sitting in the back seat for God's sake, waiting to talk to you. But if the car won't run, it's going to be a really long afternoon. Nobody wants to come over to your house to sit in the car. Not for two hours they don't. Even if you've got both Harrison Ford and Tommy Lee Jones in the back seat. Sometimes actors think they can make a play move in spite of itself. But they can't, and eventually, even though they believe in you and your talent, they get out of the car and leave you for some other vehicle, and without actors, you are really, truly stuck.

A play has to move. It has to go where it says it's going. And like a flight to Chicago, when the plane lands, you better damn well be in Chicago, or you're going to have some mighty angry people on your hands. But more on that later.

Put in still another mechanical way, a play is like a ski lift. What you want from a ski lift is to get in, ride to the top of the mountain, get out, look at the view, say "Wow," and go home. What you don't want, in a ski lift or a play, is to stop halfway up the mountain and just hang there. Nor do you want somebody to pull the shades, come on the loudspeaker, and lecture you about the politics of Kansas or tell you about their Aunt June, to whom nothing really happened, or show you pictures of their very pleasant children. Finally and worst of all, you don't want to ride a ski lift where there is no mountain. But it isn't enough to be told there is a mountain out there. No. If you have paid your money, you want to see the mountain for yourself. You want the ride. You want to go someplace you've never been and feel how things are there. And the playwright owes that to you. Obviously, no one sits down to write the great bumpy ride to nowhere, but that is what far too many plays feel like.

What is the mountain? What is a good subject for a play? This is the easy part, actually. Or should be. What are the mountains in our lives? They're the things we want but we can't have. I want to avenge my father's death. I want to go to Moscow. I want my husband not to call me his little bird. I want to marry this cute guy from this family that my family is fighting with. I want my sons to respect me. I want this guy Godot to show up. I want to be happy. I want to be king. I want to be dead. Etc. Etc. It almost doesn't matter what it is that the main character wants; it is the wanting that is the subject of the play. It is want that creates drama in both the tragic and comic forms. Not every story will make a play. Plays are not stories in any conventional, literary sense. Plays are stories about need.

A play is our journey through the main character's life from the point where we know what he wants to the point where he gets it or not. How he goes about getting it, what stands in his way, whether he deserves it or not, and whether he's happy when he gets it—these are all secondary issues. When you are thinking of writing a play, you should first fill in the blanks in this sentence. This is a play about a *blank* who wants *blank*. Force yourself to summarize your idea in one sentence. This play is about a king who wants his daughters to prove that they love him. This play is about an ex-con who wants to make something of herself. When you have this sentence, write it down on an index card and tape it to the underside of your computer, so when you wonder what the hell you're doing, you can just turn over your computer and read the card.

But the main character doesn't just want something. He *really* wants it. He wants it *now*. I mean in the next two hours. I am not exaggerating this urgency thing. One of the ugliest sights in the world is watching thirteen hundred people trapped together for two hours, all of whom have paid fifty dollars for the privilege, people who came in hopeful and happy, watching them turn on a character whose problem is that maybe he wants a little something sometime or other. No. We all know what it feels like to want things. What we want from the theater is the chance to see what happens if we ask for what we really need.

Plays are about survival. If turtles wrote plays, and risked coming together in the open to watch them, the plays would not be about the joy of crawling in the sand or memories of the happy days before mommy died. Plays by turtles would be about things you have to know if the species is to survive, where to bury the eggs so that more turtles will stand a chance of hatching. They would be about what not to eat, when to fight, and when to back down. They would be about what happens if you break the long-established rules of turtle life. Plays by turtles would contain the things the species must remember, even if they are forgotten by individual members. Anything else would not be worth your turtle time, and you would probably swim off in the middle of the thing and go eat or get laid.

Plays are about need. The main character must be aware of her need, and she must be active in her efforts to get what she needs. Given those two things, the end of the play is a snap, and a very satisfying one. The main character must either get what she needs or deal with how she can live without it.

Now occasionally some genius writes a play about more than one character. But not often. Most good plays are about one person and what that one person needs. Anybody who has ever tried to satisfy two needy children at once knows it is very hard to pay attention to two sets of needs. In life you sometimes have to do it, but in the theater you have the luxury of just considering, for two hours, the longing of one heart.

We care about the needs of one person because that is how we go through life. As one person. And when we see what someone else wants, and hear what she has to say about it, and see what she does, then we know who she is, compared to us—which is how we learn most things, I think, by comparison. Character develops by comparison too. Moment to moment, we watch the main character as if she were us. As if we wanted to be king, as if we wanted to marry Romeo. And if the writer has done her job, at the end of the play, we haven't just watched, we have actually felt what it was like to be Juliet, to be Blanche DuBois, to be Mrs. Antrobus. The playwright's task is to give the audience the experience of being someone else, of living the crucial moment in someone else's life. So how do you do that?

Well, after you identify the moment you're going to watch, then you pick the perfect place to stand and see the thing. Going back to the ski lift analogy, if you build one, you don't take people around the back of the mountain. You don't take them to a little cave about halfway up. You take them to the top. If you're going to show a whole life in two hours, you have to pick the moment from which the whole life is visible.

My play 'Night, Mother is about a woman who wants to kill herself. I could have set it in any number of moments. I could have set it at the funeral and told the whole thing in flashback. I could have set it in her imagination as she was deciding to do it. I could have set it at her brother's house when he was trying to get dressed for the funeral. But no. That would be the solemn version. Solemn is deadly. Serious is what we want. Dead serious.

'Night, Mother is about suicide. Suicide is a terrible thing. We want to know what to do if somebody we know tries to kill herself. We want to see somebody try to stop her. So I set the play in the hour and a half before Jessie kills herself, and put with her the person who had the greatest claim on that life, the person who stood the best chance of saving her. And watched what happened as Jessie tried to explain herself and make sure Mama would be all right after she died. And watched as Mama tried to find something that would work. I made it Saturday night so no one would come and interrupt them. I had Mama try to make a phone call for help but had Jessie threaten to kill herself more quickly if she did. I set up an underlying three-act structure, with Mama searching first the present, then the past, and finally the future for the solution to this puzzle. I made sure that it got harder and harder for both of them, the action escalating, the stakes getting higher and higher, and I kept the clock ticking.

Now. In the first ten minutes of the play, tell the audience what the main character wants. Do not count on them to get this by ESP or common sense. Tell them. I'm really getting mellow in my old age here. I used to say that this had to happen on page 8. But now I say page 8 to 10 is OK. The audience will give you ten minutes to get going, to fill them in on where you are, to show them you can fly this thing, and tell them where you are going. But then you have to do it. Announce the destination. Brad wants the family piano. Macbeth wants to be king. Whatever.

When the audience knows what the main character wants, they relax, they know when they can go home. The next thing they need, in order to feel comfortable and be able to follow you, is a grid, a kind of map for the world you are taking them into. They need to know how to store the information you're about to give them. Who are the main characters, who are the observers, and how are they related? Where are we, the country or the city, the past or the future, and how do things work here? Are we looking at years here, or days? Is it a sane world? How do people usually solve their problems? When we know the world, we begin to anticipate things, to fear what will happen. We begin to live in the play. We move forward in our seats, we gasp and laugh and dread the terrible end we fear is coming. Hamlet won't really kill everybody, will he? Emily isn't really going to die, is she? Dread is a fabulous thing to feel in the theater, and you can only dread the trip up the mountain if you know how high it is, how cold it is, and how unprepared you are.

Now, finally, character and plot, and how they are related. Good characters have some or all of the following: a particular way of speaking, things they think are funny, personal history (including grudges and passions), an occupation, size, gender and age, failures, secrets, ways of wasting time, delusions, weaknesses, and dreams. They have a name, and you should not start writing them until you know what it is. They have things they know how to do and things they don't. They take steps. They make mistakes. There is nothing more deadly than a passive central character except maybe a whole stage full of people who all talk alike.

I have the idea that you should be able to erase all the character names in a play and still tell who is talking. I have the idea that you shouldn't write the first page until you know how everybody talks. Like a composer who decides which instruments he will put into the piece, a playwright voices the play first. How characters speak is your first and maybe your best clue to how they think—what they do with their ideas and their time, how picky they are, how dull, how determined. And how people think is a whole lot of who they are.

And when you know who the characters are, then you know what will happen. Plot does not come from above. Plot comes from who these people are on the stage. They do what they do because they must. Or they can. Or they feel like it. But it is the characters who act, who cause the thing to move forward. The plot is nothing more than what the main character does and what the other characters do back. We try to make it look more complicated than that, but it isn't. And if it seems like a sport here, well, it feels that way sometimes. Each move the character makes takes him closer to his goal or puts him further behind. As his problems arise, and as he solves them or is defeated by them, the play moves toward its resolution, which, when we get there, must come just when we are ready for it, and must not be a surprise. We arrive at last at the top of the mountain. And it is as glorious and terrifying as we thought. It must be what we feared would happen from the start, unless it's a comedy, of course, when the end must be what we feared would never, could never happen.

Plays seem to unfold on the stage effortlessly, humorously, carried along by the ticking of the clock and the tendency of people to keep talking. But they are anything but accidental. Good plays answer the audience's questions as they ask them, but not before. They don't burden the audience with information they don't need. They do provide information, relief, and amusement as necessary.

Now to telescope the rest of what you need to know with one concluding paragraph. The language of plays cannot be exactly as it is spoken in the world, but must be slightly larger than life, so that when the actors speak it, slightly louder than normal, it can shrink a little on its way out to the audience and arrive on their ears sounding just right. Furthermore, the play is not simply what is in the lines. The play is also what is not said, what lies under the lines, and what the audience imagines during intermission. Plays are best written quickly, are derived from things that happened at least ten years ago, and if you're looking for a good idea for a play, think about some time when you were really scared. Remember that the audience doesn't care about ghosts, that if you want to cover your exposition, a good way to do it is in a fight, and a good cheap trick is to put in a character who doesn't know what's going on. Don't let the characters just stand around and talk. That's as boring on the stage as it usually is in life. If you can't figure out anything else for them to be doing, have someone spill a cup of coffee. There are certain subjects almost no one is interested in onstage. One of those is incest. Another is religion. Don't give two characters names that start with the same letter. A big speech works best if the character doesn't want to give it. Don't write big roles for child actors, as they are very hard to find and they can't rehearse a full day. When somebody wants to direct your play, the important question to ask them is what they like about it. Don't sign a contract without talking to the Dramatists Guild, and . . .

Everything else will be covered in the advanced course.

On Leaving Things Out

Francine Prose

Some years ago a friend called to invite me to contribute to an anthology in which a number of writers were each being asked to write a brief introduction to his or her favorite story by his or her favorite writer, not counting him or herself. A favorite dead writer, I understood my friend to mean, though in retrospect I don't remember whether this qualification was stated or implied. Knowing that if I hesitated even for a moment I would never be able to answer the ridiculous question—which was my favorite story?—I said I wanted to write about a story by Isaac Babel, or if that proved impossible, a story by Bruno Schulz.

My friend hesitated. Well, it seemed that an older, more famous writer had also expressed an interest in introducing an Isaac Babel story. My friend said he would get back to me.

Two years went by. The projected anthology went through a number of editors, during which time the older, more famous writer apparently lost interest in writing about Isaac Babel or any other dead writer, because the message my friend left on my answering machine said the anthology was proceeding on schedule, and could I please send my essay in by the end of the week?

Once more I was just as glad not to have time to vacillate among the dozens of Babel stories I might have chosen. Should I pick "Crossing into Poland," which may well be the most powerful, perfect, and shocking three pages I have ever read, or "My First Goose," surely the most beautiful story ever written about war and the source and mystery of violence? Finally I chose "Guy de Maupassant," the story I know best, almost by heart, the one I've most often taught, and the one I believe to be so transcendent and enigmatic that nothing I could say about it could ever reduce or spoil it. Here, then, is the preface I wrote for my friend's anthology:

> If mysteries, by definition, cannot be explained, the next best thing—or better thing—is to recreate them.
>
> Isaac Babel's "Guy de Maupassant" does precisely that. This brilliant story addresses the linked or parallel mysteries of art and of sex. By its shocking conclusion, readers will have experienced something beyond the cerebral, something visceral, inexpressible, the shivery mix of pure clarity and dizzying confusion that we feel in the presence of mystery, and that both art and sex can provide.
>
> Penniless, gifted, dreamy, the story's young narrator is a perfect Babel hero: the world is denying and promising him everything at once. Housed with a struggling literature teacher in a "yellow, frozen, evil-smelling" quarter of St. Petersburg, he's hired to help a rich man's passionate, plump, somewhat dopey daughter with her translation from the French of de Maupassant's work. Their literary labors are interrupted and augmented by the distractions of proximity, fantasy, and flesh. And after a night of wine, flirting, and translating one of the French writer's steamier stories . . . our hero goes home, opens a biography of de Maupassant, and has a moment in which Babel gives us one of the most meaningful, complicated, beautiful, troubling, and absolutely irreducible passages in all of literature.
>
> But plot summary doesn't come close to touching a Babel story. Even among writers, Babel was a fanatic, a tireless reviser who would do fifty versions of a phrase and whose ranting about paragraphing and word choice, as reported in Paustovsky's *Years of Hope*, should be embroidered on a sampler and hung over every desk. "Guy de Maupassant," too, is full of writing advice—"No steel can pierce the human heart with such force as a period put

just at the right place"—pronouncements in which we hear Babel boasting and scaring himself, both at once.

Knowing that every word has been put on trial fifty times does make one stop and wonder why it was chosen, and so often spared. Having written that way, Babel rewards you for reading that way. "Guy de Maupassant" has amazing details, astonishing descriptions, and studying it detail by detail, word by word, does bring us closer to the inner workings that make the story tick, or at least closer than we get from plot summary, above.

But not even close reading will take us all the way to the heart of the story—to which there is no access, except through some understanding that surpasses not merely the literary but the rational as well.

That is why I started by talking about a mystery.

There is much to be said about "Guy de Maupassant," about art and sex, literature, death, complication, the dark side of art and sex and literature, knowledge, experience . . . etc. I've seen writers start to hyperventilate before giving up on trying to explain why Babel was such a great writer.

But finally there is nothing to say. We can only reread the story—as if this time, at last, we will seize and reduce what has eluded us before.

"Guy de Maupassant" is great art and defies all explanation while teasing us with elusive hints of higher information. This story explodes the silly idea that there can be any limit on how much larger and deeper something can be than the sum of its separate parts.

Even as I was writing this, I was uncomfortably aware of several things—perhaps the most important things—that I was leaving out.

The most obvious omission was the rest of Babel's advice on revision, the chapter from *Years of Hope* that for reasons of space and possibly copyright I could hardly reproduce in its entirety, though it alone proves beyond any doubt what a great writer and great fanatic Babel really was. It is the most extreme and lyrical passage I know on the subject of revision, one which my unfortunate writing students have had to listen to again and again, and they no doubt count themselves lucky because I've never insisted they memorize it.

The circumstances surrounding Babel's monologue involve a visit by Paustovsky to Babel's study, where he spotted a towering stack of manuscript pages and allowed himself to hope that Babel, who (only!) wrote short fiction, was finally writing a novel. Babel was quick to disenchant him; the pages represented twenty-two drafts of a single story:

"So there it is," said Babel, stooping short-sightedly over his manuscript. "I work like a pack mule, but it's my own choice. I'm like a galley slave who's chained for life to his oar but who loves the oar. Everything about it. Every grain of wood he's polished with his hands. If you use enough elbow grease, even the coarsest wood gets to look like ivory. That's what we have to do with words. . . . Warm it and polish it with your hand, and it glows like a jewel.

"But I meant to tell you all I do, in the right order. The first version of a story is terrible. All in bits and pieces tied together with boring 'link passages' as dry as old rope. . . . It yaps at you, it's clumsy, helpless, toothless.

"That's where the real work begins. I go over each sentence, time and again. I start by cutting all the words it can do without. You have to keep your eye on the job because words are very sly, the rubbishy ones go into hiding and you have to dig them out—repetitions, synonyms, things that simply don't mean anything.

"After that I type the story and let it lie for two or three days. If I can hold out. Then I check it again, sentence by sentence and word by word. And again I find a lot of rubbish I missed the first time. So I make another copy, and another—as many as I have to, until I've cleaned it all up and there's not a speck of dirt left.

"But that's not all! When I've done the cleaning up, I go over every image, metaphor, comparison, to see if they are fresh and accurate. If you can't find the right adjective for a noun, leave it alone. Let the noun stand by itself.

"A comparison must be as accurate as a slide rule, and as natural as the smell of fennel. Oh, I forgot—before I take out the rubbish, I break up the text into shorter sentences. The more full stops the better. I'd like to have that passed as a law. Not more than one idea and one image to one sentence. Never be afraid of full stops. Actually, my own sentences are too short—that's because of my asthma. I can't talk for long. The longer the sentence the more I get short of breath.

"I take out all the participles and adverbs I can. Participles are heavy, angular, they destroy the rhythm. They grate like tanks going over rubble. Three participles to one sentence, and you kill the language. . . . Adverbs are lighter. They can even lend you wings in a way. But too many of them make the language spineless, it starts mioaling. . . . A noun needs only one adjective, the choicest. Only a genius can afford two adjectives to one noun.

"The breaking up into paragraphs and punctuation has to be done properly but only for the effect on the reader. A set of dead rules is no good. A new paragraph is a wonderful thing. It lets you quietly change the rhythm, and it can be like a flash of lightning that shows the same landscape from a different aspect. There are writers, even good ones, who scatter paragraphs and punctuation marks all over the place. They can write good prose, but it has an air of muddle and carelessness because of this. . . .

"Line is as important in prose as in an engraving. It has to be clear and hard. . . . There can be as much difference between the first and last version of a book as between a greasy bit of packing paper and Botticelli's *Primavera*.

"It really is slave labour," I said. "A man should think twenty times before he decides to become a writer.

"But the most important thing of all," said Babel, "is not to kill the story by working on it. Or else all your labour has been in vain. It's like walking a tightrope. Well, there it is. . . . We ought all to take an oath not to mess up our job."

The other obvious absence from my introduction was, of course, the story itself, which my friend assured me would follow my introduction in the published anthology. I tried (without ruining the story) to reveal only as much of its plot as was necessary to talk about its mystery and meaning.

But since I have come to believe that there is no way of ruining this great work of art, I want to read you the section I was alluding to in my introduction, a few paragraphs from the end of the story, so as to make clearer (as if there were any way of making clear) what I was trying to describe: the mystery and ambiguity that transcend and surpass our inadequate powers of reason and make the story's conclusion so unforgettable and so haunting. (You should know that Raïsa is the woman with whom our hero is translating de Maupassant and that Kazantsev is the teacher with whom he lodges.)

Night had blocked the path of my famished youth with a bottle of Muscatel '83 and twenty-nine books, twenty-nine bombs stuffed with pity, genius and passion. I sprang up, knocking over the chair and banging against the shelf. The twenty-nine volumes crashed to the floor, their pages flew open, they fell on their edges . . . and the white mare of my fate went on at a walking pace.

"You are funny," growled Raïsa.

I left the granite house on the Moyka between eleven and twelve, before the sisters and the husband returned from the theater. I was sober and could have walked a chalk line, but it was pleasanter to stagger, so I swayed from side to side, singing in a language I had just invented. Through the tunnels of the streets bounded by lines of street lights the steamy fog billowed. Monsters roared behind the boiling walls. The roads amputated the legs of those walking on them.

Kazantsev was asleep when I got home. He slept sitting up, his thin legs extended in their felt boots. The canary fluff rose on his head. He had fallen asleep by the stove bending over a volume of *Don Quixote,* the edition of 1624. On the title-page of the book was a dedication to the Duc de Broglie. I got into bed quietly, so as not to wake Kazantsev; moved the lamp close to me and began to read a book by Edouard Maynial on Guy de Maupassant's life and work.

Kazantsev's lips moved; his head kept keeling over.

That night I learned from Edouard Maynial that Maupassant was born in 1850, the child of a Normandy gentleman and Laure Lepoiteven, Flaubert's cousin. He was twenty-five when he was first attacked by congenital syphilis. His productivity and *joie de vivre* withstood the onsets of the disease. At first he suffered from headaches and fits of hypochondria. Then the specter of blindness arose before him. His sight weakened. He became suspicious of everyone, unsociable and pettily quarrelsome. He struggled furiously, dashed about the Mediterranean in a yacht, fled to Tunis, Morocco, Central Africa . . . and wrote ceaselessly. He attained fame, and at forty years of age cut his throat, lost a great deal of blood, yet lived through it. He was then put away in a madhouse. There he crawled about on his hands and knees, devouring his own excrement. The last line in his hospital report read: *Monsieur de Maupassant va s'animaliser.* He died at the age of forty-two, his mother surviving him.

I read the book to the end and got out of bed. The fog came close to the window, the world was hidden from me. My heart contracted as the foreboding of some essential truth touched me with light fingers.

Only now do I realize: something else has been left out of my introduction, something I should have begun with, perhaps: the facts of Babel's biography, most of which were of course hidden from him when he wrote "Guy de Maupassant," as our lives are hidden from us but may appear in our work in prescient, spooky, and baffling ways, long before we could have known them. Here are a few quotations from Babel's autobiographical sketch:

I was born in 1894 in Odessa in the Moldavanka district, the son of a Jewish shopkeeper. My father insisted that I study Hebrew, the Bible and the Talmud until I was sixteen. My life at home was hard because from morning to night they forced me to study a great many subjects. I rested in school.

Later, after graduation, I found myself in Kiev and then in 1915 in Petersburg. I didn't have a residence permit, and had to avoid the police, living on Pushkin Street in a cellar rented from a bedraggled, drunken waiter. Also in 1915 I began to take my writing around to editorial offices, but I was always thrown out. All the editors tried to persuade me to get a job in a store, but I didn't listen to them. Then at the end of 1916 I happened to meet Maxim Gorky. I owe everything to this meeting, and to this day I speak his name with love and reverence. . . . He taught me extremely important things and sent me into the world at a time when it was clear that my two or three tolerable attempts as a young man were, at best, successful by accident, that I would not get anywhere with literature, and that I wrote amazingly badly.

For seven years—from 1917 to 1924—I was out in the world. During this time I was a soldier on the Rumanian front; then I served in the Cheka . . . and in the First Cavalry. . . . I was production supervisor in the 7th Soviet Publishing House . . . a reporter in Petersburg and Tiflis, etc. Only in 1923 did I learn how to express my thoughts clearly and concisely. . . . Therefore I consider that my literary career started at the beginning of 1924.

What Babel leaves out (or expects us to know) was that he volunteered for military service and that the unit he rode with—and that became the subject of many of his strongest stories—was the infamous Red Cavalry, the notoriously violent Cossacks, the historical enemies of the Jews, responsible for the bloodiest pogroms against the Jews of Russia. Those first few stories he published in 1924 made him instantly famous, a fame that would be his undoing under the Stalinist regime. Unable to write what the Party required, he wrote less and less, and in a bitterly ironic speech to the Party Congress he described himself as a Master of the Art of Silence. He was arrested in 1939 and disappeared and died under unexplained circumstances in Siberia, or in prison.

᪥

Months after I'd handed in my essay on "Guy de Maupassant," I discovered the most serious thing that I'd left out of my preface. I was talking to a friend who'd contributed to the same volume. She'd written her introduction two years before, when we were first asked, perhaps because no other writer claimed the Katherine Mansfield story she'd picked, or because she was more diligent, or possibly because she had understood our mission to be quite different; it was her (probably accurate) impression that we were meant to describe the circumstances under which we'd first read the story we'd chosen.

Right then, I knew that I'd left out everything, because as soon as she said that, I remembered exactly when I'd first read "Guy de Maupassant." And though it would take a while until I thought I understood why (and again the truth may be hidden from me), I intuited that there was something about the summer when I first discovered Babel that not only had some relation with Babel's story but with how I became a writer, and with why I wrote so badly for so long.

It was the summer of my sophomore year in college. I was living at home in New York and taking two courses at Columbia. One was a fiction writing class (because I'd secretly decided to become a writer) and the other was an introduction to studio architecture (because my secret decision wasn't so secret, and my parents must have hoped that something might still persuade me to take up a lucrative or at least useful profession).

My teacher was a nice man who later became mildly well known for his long experimental novels in the style (more or less) of James Joyce. He wasn't interested in our work (in retrospect I can see why) but preferred describing the eccentricities and exploits of the Beat and Black Mountain writers he knew, his ex-wives and drinking buddies. Looking back, I wonder if he told us all this to prove that he wasn't some loser earning next to nothing for teaching a summer course, but instead an artist with an exciting bohemian life that resumed the minute class ended and he practically ran out the door. Strangely, it never occurred to us to resent his lack of enthusiasm for our writing, nor to think less of him for the way he'd found to earn extra money. I sat in worshipful silence as he spoke of the life I dreamed of leading.

That is, a hollow husk sat there, pretending to be me, while my real self was elsewhere, somewhere, mired in darkness. That summer, my boyfriend was in California, and without him I felt I did not exist except when, like the tablet of salt the sorcerer places on the tongue of a zombie, his rare letters and phone calls restored me briefly to life. (Since then, I have written about this state of believing oneself a shadow in the absence of some guy, though at the time it was all too scary and close for me to acknowledge that I was in a condition like that.)

The part of me that pretended to be there was a truly deranged obsessive, brooding on the fact that, only that summer, a small but disturbing number of New Yorkers were being beaned by cornices and chunks of masonry crumbling off the tops of buildings. Why was I so certain that this would be my fate that I often walked with my head tilted back and tripped over curbs and hydrants?

The other thing that happened was that, out in Chicago, Richard Speck had just murdered eight nurses in a case that I was also obsessed with, perhaps because (in my walking coma) I identified with the hapless young women, too passive to defend themselves against the killer they so outnumbered.

This was what I thought about as I sat in the sunlit classroom and laughed at my teacher's gossipy anecdotes and wrote down his reading suggestions, works he recommended with a passion I'd never heard in my college literature classes, until his pride in a daily life that loved art and defied convention distracted and engaged me, and I suddenly felt quite fully present and calm and briefly forgot my morbid worries.

What I am trying to say is that my entire experience of that summer took place along the blurry line dividing darkness and light that the narrator of "Guy de Maupassant" walks throughout the story and crosses several times and finally sees, at the story's conclusion. And yet I didn't see that, though I was voraciously (and in a state of shock) reading Isaac Babel, who was one of the writers my teacher recommended. I read Babel on the subway traveling back and forth to class, and I remember very clearly when I first read the end of "Guy de Maupassant."

Something must have shown on my face because I looked up and noticed that several people—on a New York subway!—were staring at me with evident concern.

Everything that happened that summer walked that same razor edge. I used to ride the subway partway downtown with my teacher and several students, talking art, talking literature, until I got off and changed trains at 42nd Street, when I had to go through several long and dim, semideserted tunnels that I would be extremely anxious about even entering now. Once, in such a tunnel, a man in a shiny gray suit came at me and grabbed my breast. I gasped, and then he gasped. He seemed more shocked than I was. We hurried away in opposite directions, and when I breathlessly reported the incident to the nearest transit cop, he said he was sorry, he couldn't help, and I saw that the person I'd mistaken for a cop was just a tall boy, an Eagle Scout.

Meanwhile I was trying to write. I was writing a terrible story, and one of the reasons it was so vile (besides the fact that I couldn't write a decent sentence and didn't know the first thing about the English language, or any other language) was that I hadn't learned the lessons that the summer and Babel were trying to teach me, so that what I was leaving out—again—was the most important part.

The story I was trying to write was based on an incident that occurred in my neighborhood when I was eleven or twelve. The boy who lived in the house behind mine was playing in his backyard with his friends, and after a while they called me over to be an audience for what they were doing. What they were doing was tying a firecracker to a wounded blue jay that couldn't fly, and as I watched, also unable to move, they lit the fuse and the bird exploded.

In my story the girl runs back to her house and weeps and weeps and weeps in horror at the sufferings of the helpless and the cruelty of humanity in general, and boys in particular, and the sudden, violent, irrevocable loss of innocence (her own).

But in fact that wasn't what happened at all. The truth was that I adored those boys, my neighbor and his friends. And the real truth was that I was less revolted by their cruel act than aroused and flattered that they'd called me over to watch it. My own emotions horrified me as much as the boys' cruelty. I found it all extremely confusing and altogether less simple and safe than what the girl in the story experienced. In fact I didn't run home at all but stayed because I liked being near the boys and was curious to see what they would do next.

What they did next was get tired of me, and they laughed and ran away.

So one of the reasons my story was so bad was that I'd left out the real emotion. Or I'd lied about the emotion—that is, I'd pretended that the experience was like that of the narrator in the Babel story, but only the translating, the flirting, the good wine and great writing, and not the part about de Maupassant going insane and eating shit and turning into an animal. I was trying to have the correct—the nice—response, and in the process left out the genuine one, the unlovely and unacceptable emotion that was far more interesting, complicated, and human.

I have heard it said that writing fiction is less about what the writer puts in than about what is left out. (Mostly I've heard this said by misguided Hemingway fans and by those who have grotesquely misread the stories of Raymond Carver.) The point, I think, is not to leave things out but to include it all (if we think back to Babel's advice) in as few words as possible.

The greatness of the Babel story is in its brave embrace of light and darkness, its awareness of the grinning skull beneath the smile of pleasure, and in what Babel knew about the danger of seeing one without the other: about the difference between leaving things out and the comforting lies of omission that will eventually turn us all into genteel, obedient masters of the art of silence.

The Figure of Vacancy

Wyatt Prunty

In Flannery O'Connor's "A Good Man Is Hard to Find," the grandmother is the first to comment upon the blankness of the sky. Later the Misfit says, "Don't see no sun but don't see no cloud neither." In Peter Taylor's "A Wife of Nashville," Helen Ruth stands silently behind a tea cart and looks into the dark recesses of her living room as she prepares to explain to the men of her family why Jess McGehee had to lie about leaving. The blank sky of the one story and a prolonged silence in the other are only two of many representations of despair, but they provide a good place to begin thinking about the figure of vacancy.

For Flannery O'Connor and Peter Taylor, narrative leads to gaps. These may appear as a nondescript sky or the recesses of a room, or they may take the form of a zero unwittingly added to a date or a lie added to a story. However they come about, these vacancies refute normal expectations and open new perspectives.

Flannery O'Connor introduces the raw realities of life in rural Georgia then uses wit, caricature, and cartoonlike violence to void normal expectations and achieve situations more complicated than ordinary description uncovers. Not made to face what frequently are O'Connor's violent extremes, Peter Taylor's characters nevertheless place one another in extremis so the complexities of their lives are put in relief. For both writers this is done by pairing characters, pairing their situations and actions so the ordinary closure we expect from a story is broken open and what follows is the figure of vacancy.

Compared to O'Connor's, Peter Taylor's characters march by in rounded and unexaggerated form. Characterization follows the conventions of literary realism and avoids the religious allegory of O'Connor's fiction. The people who most often populate Taylor's stories are individuals of substantial means and reliable judgment who find themselves operating by codes that no longer hold sway, as they stand politely isolated while their world disintegrates around them. But Taylor's gentlefolk do share one important trait with O'Connor's rustics, and that is vacancy. Well-heeled and ruminative as they are, Taylor's characters parallel O'Connor's when they confront their own bleak ends. For Taylor's people, despair results from individual and cultural blind spots. While O'Connor pushes her characters to absolute ends, Taylor's characters experience neither the violence nor the terror that O'Connor raises, but they too are misfits. They stand before equally powerful forms of vacancy, muted as those forms may be by the mores of Chatham, Thornton, Nashville, and Memphis.

The people who populate O'Connor's "A Good Man Is Hard to Find" are flat yet exaggerated individuals facing their own meanness and mortality. Pressed to a different sort of absolute, Helen Ruth and the other characters in Taylor's "A Wife of Nashville" do not experience the violence that besets the grandmother and her family in "A Good Man Is Hard to Find," but Taylor's characters are stranded by elements in their lives that are as empty and inexplicable as the blank sky that characterizes the meeting between the grandmother and the Misfit.

O'Connor and Taylor have numerous stories in which the protagonist and other characters are like the ironical "self" Kierkegaard describes as seeking to be that "which [it] is not." It is a self caught three ways at once: in the despair of not knowing who one is, the despair of not willing to be oneself, and the despair of willing to be someone other than oneself. Any individual who is in one of these situations is automatically in the other two as well. One cannot will to be himself or herself without knowing who that self is. And since the will is a given, if the self does not know who it is, it must will to be someone other than itself. And so on, laughably or lamentably, around the three sides.

Flannery O'Connor's copy of Walter Lowrie's translation of Kierkegaard's *The Sickness Unto Death* contains a marginal notation that appears after Kierkegaard's description of the three-sided despair outlined above. The section O'Connor marked discusses the philistine's lack of imagination and the fact that "reality helps" alleviate this lack by providing "terrors which transcend the *parrot-wisdom* of trivial experiences" (italics mine). Remembering "A Good Man Is Hard to Find," one thinks not only of Bailey's parrot shirt, later returned from his dead body, but also of his terror as he stands paralyzed in a runner's starting position. O'Connor's solution to "parrot wisdom" (and here her genius for radicalizing clichés comes to mind) is to increase the stakes, causing the philistine to despair more and more, until the condition of despair is starkly visible. (Various examples come to mind: Mr. Head's saying he's lost at the end of "The Artificial Nigger"; Joy trapped in the hayloft at the end of "Good Country People"; Julian running for help at the end of "Everything That Rises Must Converge"; Mr. Fortune realizing that he has killed his granddaughter and namesake at the end of "A View of the Woods"; and, of course, in "A Good Man Is Hard to Find" the grandmother witnessing the sequential murders of her entire family.)

For Kierkegaard, there are gradations of despair, but the worst form is not knowing one is in despair. Until the end of "A Good Man Is Hard to Find," the grandmother's smug pretensions to gentility and her manipulative assumptions about goodness reveal that she does not recognize her real condition. She is a finished example of the philistine Kierkegaard describes and that O'Connor noted with her marginal lining in *The Sickness Unto Death*. In O'Connor's understanding, "parrot-wisdom" can lead only to vacancy, so that is where the real action occurs, where characters in despair are either sealed as themselves or erased permanently. An instance of this is the grandmother's hackneyed lie about Sherman and the secret panel that steers the family toward the Misfit. But later, sitting in the ditch in which the family's car has overturned, the grandmother reaches out to the Misfit and articulates who she is by saying who he is, one of her "babies."

O'Connor's and Taylor's characters live around empty places, but where they live they encounter a lot of company, and they are defined by their relations to others. Each is at once a discrete individual with selfish concerns and an extensional self too: a mother, father, brother, son, daughter. Each is a subjective and autobiographical self, and each is an objective and biographical self. Vacancy results from failure to recognize the objective and biographical side of the self.

The grandmother in "A Good Man Is Hard to Find" begins as a petty manipulator of the truth. She wants the family to vacation in geographically contracted "east Tennessee," where she says the children will have a chance to become "broad." She uses news accounts of the Misfit's murders to push her case. At this point in the story there is nothing grand about the grandmother. She is the one who vainly thinks her dressing well ensures that anyone finding her dead on the highway will know she was a lady. By the end of the story, however, this same character grows into her name, becoming a grand (that is, full grown) mother.

In Peter Taylor's "A Wife of Nashville," Helen Ruth recognizes her kinship with her maid Jess McGehee as she gradually realizes the long-term vacancy that has characterized both their lives in Nashville. The social and economic differences between the white wife of a businessman and her black servant are vast, but by the story's end it is clear these are not the real source of the trouble. After Jess's departure at the end of the story, Helen Ruth stands before her husband and sons and falls silent. She is taking a moment to gather all the normative patterns of thought and behavior from which everyone who is of Nashville suffers. "My dears, don't you see how it was for Jess?" she asks. But of course they do not see because they cannot see how it is even for themselves.

In each of these stories the protagonist mediates between a subjective and objective self. And the despair that all of the characters experience derives from not knowing who they are, not willing to be themselves, thus willing to be someone other than themselves. Despair is this three-sided place that the reader encounters in the figure of vacancy.

In "A Good Man Is Hard to Find," after the grandmother and her family have stopped for lunch, the otherwise passive mother of John Wesley, June Star, and the baby, a woman whose face is "as broad and innocent as a cabbage," puts "a dime in the machine and play[s] 'The Tennessee Waltz,'" while her children, husband, and mother-in-law wait for their "orders" to be filled. This is the one time the mother shows enough energy to distinguish herself from her loud and willful family. The edge readers recognize in what she does results from the fact that prior to the trip the grandmother had been "seizing" every opportunity to "change Bailey's mind" so the family would vacation in "east Tennessee," where the grandmother inflatedly hopes to "visit some of her connections." The mother's decision to play "The Tennessee Waltz" reminds the grandmother that she failed to get her way, and she responds.

The grandmother "ask[s] Bailey if he would like to dance," turning the song's opening line, "I was dancing with my darling," into a claim on her son. After Bailey "glare[s] at her," she reasons that he lacks her "naturally sunny disposition," and O'Connor says "the grandmother's brown eyes were very bright" as she "swayed her head from side to side and pretended she was dancing in her chair." Bailey glares, the grandmother's eyes are "bright," and the internal fires build. The one title for two very different Tennessee waltzes creates a gap that prefigures the opening among the pines where the grandmother and the Misfit will pair off.

The narrator in "The Tennessee Waltz" tells us he was "dancing" with his "darlin'" to "The Tennessee Waltz," an older tune named but never heard. Added to the song about a missing song, there is the grandmother's confusion about gentility and the good, each of these a kind of vacancy, just as the Misfit's date for his father's death, "nineteen ought nineteen," 19019, adds "ought" to the date, suggesting *nought, cipher,* or *zero.* Each of these figures represents disjunction and vacancy. There is no such year as "nineteen ought nineteen"; the grandmother's clichés about gentility and goodness are hollow; the lie she tells about the secret panel creates the opportunity (or the vacuum) for the Misfit to enter the action; and "The Tennessee Waltz" named is not "The Tennessee Waltz" played in the story, just as the house the grandmother entices her family to detour and see is not along their way in Georgia but behind them in east Tennessee.

"A Good Man Is Hard to Find" is constructed around gaps. The story's title, a cliché that becomes the chilling truth, is taken from another unheard song, and it too operates as a kind of cipher—vacant as a platitude, thus waiting to be filled by new meaning. The grandmother tells Red Sammy he is a good man, and he accepts that as the truth. Until the Misfit appears, the grandmother's sentimental veneer covers the action. When she tries to apply it to the Misfit, however, he thwarts her, saying, "Nome, I ain't a good man."

The family has stopped outside Timothy, Georgia, and the grandmother echoes Paul's Second Epistle to Timothy, where Paul encourages his friend to "endure hardness, as a good soldier." Red Sammy describes an episode in which he trusted two men who asked for credit but didn't pay. "Now why did I do that?" Sammy asks. "Because you're a good man!" the grandmother tells him. Sammy's response is to say, "Yes'm, I suppose so." O'Connor adds that Red Sammy is "struck with this answer." That is, he is surprised but accepting of its truth. A dozen or so lines later, after the Misfit has been discussed, Red Sammy is still thinking about what the grandmother said before and volunteers, "A good man is hard to find." By now the grandmother's good man, who will be extremely hard on her, has begun making shadows in the background.

The Misfit is an ironical but not totally negative agent, at least not for the grandmother. He is the means by which she is killed, but O'Connor sees him as the grandmother's salvation too. The Misfit is an agent by which O'Connor revives a truth long buried in the grandmother's clichéd understanding of what good means. The Misfit's view is that "She would have been a good woman . . . if it had been somebody there to shoot her every minute of her life." This comical but harsh statement is a variation on O'Connor's ultimate view of the grandmother. As Kierkegaard suggested, only terror will save her from her philistinism.

The Misfit limits knowledge to his own brand of empiricism, a product of materialism and rationalism that he seems to have absorbed by osmosis. O'Connor would say he got it from the air he breathed. In Timothy, Paul describes one who is "ever learning and never able to come to the knowledge of the truth," an apt description of the Misfit, who in his literal-mindedness, perhaps a parody of gnostic pride, remains a skeptic. For O'Connor, the Misfit's desire to reduce faith to knowledge is just as incongruous and freakish as the way he fuses brutality with manners. He is at once an absolutist and a doubting Thomas whose self-contradictory understanding leads to his despairing judgment that "It's no real pleasure in life. . . . No pleasure but meanness."

O'Connor sees a knotted relationship between the Misfit and the grandmother. He is a cold-blooded killer who possesses reason and honesty the grandmother lacks. His insistence that he see in order to know contributes to both his absolutism and his nihilism. The grandmother is much too interested in her smug comfort to go as far as the Misfit does. The Misfit would never sentimentalize a situation or flatter someone. Sentimentality and flattery are the grandmother's currency.

The Misfit and the grandmother meet in a clearing stark enough to represent both of them. It is a vacant place suitable for the Misfit's different levels of denial: the unacknowledged fact that he killed his father, his reducing belief to experience, and his asserting that there is no "pleasure," *i.e.*, joy, "in life." The clearing also is a place suitable for the grandmother's repeated denial: her series of lies—lies to herself about gentility, race, and poverty; her "sunny disposition"; the integrity of the past; her cat's affection for her; and, after she realizes she was wrong about the house with the secret panel, her tacit lie in not correcting herself, which along with her hiding the cat, causes the family's accident. What fills the vacancy created by these lies is the Misfit.

When the Misfit appears, the grandmother is the one who recognizes him and thus ensures another level of denial, that he will have to kill the family in order to cover his tracks. The clearing surrounded by menacing pines under the featureless Georgia sky, through which the wind blows like an "insuck of breath," stands figuratively for the two main characters in the story. The two meet. Yet out of all the negatives they bring to that scene there is one positive, and that is the change that occurs in the grandmother.

Vacancy can be a vacation, vacated office, or self-vacancy. As mentioned before, the grandmother is never referred to by any name other than the one that defines her office, yet she vacates that role until the story's end. The grandmother has developed a set of comfortable assertions by which she holds off the despair that characterizes her. Until she is terrorized into doubting this structure and rejects it, she is locked in the despair of not knowing who she is. But the grandmother is not alone in this.

The story begins with Bailey reading the sports section of the paper. Later, when he is given the opportunity for his own moment of physical courage and athletic prowess, Bailey fails entirely. He leaves the story just as passively as he entered it. He knows the family is in a "terrible predicament," but his eyes are "as blue and intense as the parrots in his shirt." That is, he is cognizant in a secondary way, similar to a parrot. He can repeat, but in his "parrot-speech" he cannot originate ideas or take action. He can see, but he cannot act; therefore he "remains[s] perfectly still," and when he is ushered off, he calls the grandmother "Mama."

In "A Good Man Is Hard to Find," various secondary pairings lay the groundwork for the vacancy that is created when the story's two main characters come together. The two songs entitled "The Tennessee Waltz," and the gap, literally the "ought," in the date the Misfit gives for his father's death, "nineteen ought nineteen," ready the reader for when the grandmother and her counterpart, the Misfit, meet. And there are other preparations. One comes early in the story. It is the grandmother's observation about the weather for the family's trip: "She said she thought it was going to be a good day for driving, neither too hot nor too cold," echoing St. John the Divine's phrase, "thou art neither cold nor hot," which is the grandmother's own tepid condition, though the Misfit will take care of that. His coldness will cause her heat.

At the beginning of the story, the reader accepts what the grandmother says, that the weather is "good . . . for driving" because it is "neither too hot nor too cold." Later, when he cannot think of anything to say, the Misfit makes a chorus of this by observing, "Ain't a cloud in the sky. . . . Don't see no sun but don't see no cloud neither." And when he is describing his time in jail the Misfit "again" looks "up . . . at the cloudless sky." As Hiram and Bobby Lee take June Star, her mother, and the baby into the woods, the omniscient narrator observes that "There was not a cloud in the sky nor any sun." And, finally, after the grandmother has been shot, we see her "in a puddle of blood . . . her face smiling up at the cloudless sky." In O'Connor's fiction, the featureless sky is a frequent image for vacancy in the world below.

The trip begins with the grandmother's checking the mileage on the odometer, which warns readers of the empty hours ahead. Then she reviews how she is dressed, concluding that if she were found "dead on the highway" anyone "would know at once that she was a lady." The grandmother dramatizes the emptiness of the family's vacation. Noting that they left "Atlanta at eight forty-five with the mileage on the car at 55890," she shows readers just how tedious things can become. Further emphasizing the oppressiveness of the situation, the grandmother writes her observation down, thinking "it would be interesting to say how many miles they had been when they got back." Nothing could be less interesting. But the grandmother continues in this vein, noting that "It took them twenty minutes to reach the outskirts of the city."

The indifferent sky and the wind through the pines combine to frame the Augustinian battle between the Misfit's coldness (his decision to rely only on himself: "I don't want no hep") and the grandmother's eventual intense heat, her turn toward help when she says, "Jesus, Jesus." The Misfit thinks she is cursing, but O'Connor intends this as the grandmother's moment of grace. The grandmother reaches out to her murderer, identifying him as one of her babies because now she is a grand mother, as now, for her, the Misfit really is a good man.

The violence and sadism in this story and others by O'Connor deserve further attention, but the point intended is that the grandmother's encounter with the Misfit brings her to the "good" as O'Connor believes it really exists. Before, the grandmother just parroted this idea. Gone are the grandmother's contentions that the Misfit is "a good man" because he is "not a bit common" and that he has "good blood," both of these stemming from the grandmother's mistaking social standing for good character, a confusion similar to Julian's social relativism in "Everything That Rises Must Converge." At the end of her story, O'Connor's grandmother demonstrates love, however briefly, even for her own murderer. For once nothing is vacated; she acts on the basis of who she is. Her will is aligned with her identity. O'Connor's action has pushed what "good" means beyond where the philistine grandmother would otherwise leave it.

"A Good Man Is Hard to Find" is one of a number of O'Connor stories in which the controlling figure is invisible. Created by various kinds of pairing, the story's center is an opening out between two sides of one condition, despair. The grandmother and the Misfit meet in a gap where something is bound to happen. In the protean landscapes of O'Connor's stories, characters are matched and create an opening. They are simultaneously likened and differentiated in a process that reveals their external relationships as much as their internal feelings and aspirations. There are Mr. Head and Nelson, Mr. Fortune and Mary Fortune Pitts, the mothers and sons in "Everything That Rises Must Converge," Rufus Johnson and Sheppard in "The Lame Shall Enter First," and other matches populating the vacant places where O'Connor's characters meet.

In "A Wife of Nashville," Helen Ruth's despair is figured by the series of maids who work for her. The servants are paired with Helen Ruth, and in their successive employment they identify her progress in coming to terms with being "of" Nashville. The "of" used in the story's title indicates both belonging and separation, as in "of that family" and "eased of pain." The preposition represents an opening or vacant spot. Helen Ruth is characterized by her relation to Nashville and paired with her maids, who share her predicament there. To jump ahead momentarily, the sense of belonging-separation that characterizes Helen Ruth's situation in the story can be seen in the scrapbook and the movie magazines that Jess McGehee, the fourth and most compelling maid to work for the family, keeps in her room. These objects are projections of and consolations for what she cannot have, not even among the family members with whom she lives and to whom she is so loyal.

Helen Ruth realizes her kinship with Jess McGehee in a move that recognizes the displacement they both experience. The social and economic differences between the two are pronounced on one level and beside the point on another, where their roles leave them with the task of nurturing members of the male cast that simultaneously places and displaces them. At the story's conclusion, Jess tells a lie, creating one kind of vacancy in order to escape another. That is the only means she has to extricate herself from the family. What Helen Ruth understands about Jess's predicament, and that her husband and sons miss, is the constriction created by the mores of Nashville.

During a closing scene that reinforces the isolation of Helen Ruth's existence, even in her own home, she stands before her husband and sons and tries to explain why Jess had to use one lie in order to free herself from another. Helen Ruth has known for several days that Jess and her friend Mary plan to take the bus to California, where they hope to get jobs and live near the movie world of Hollywood that so fascinates them. What Helen Ruth has to tell the men in her family is the aggregate of her years of experience as "a" wife "of" Nashville, with all the social strata, the inclusions and exclusions, that Peter Taylor has already unfolded in the story.

Midway through "A Good Man Is Hard to Find," the scene in the Tower Restaurant produces "The Tennessee Waltz," a song about a song—reportage by one song about another that we do not hear, which reminds us of the gap between the two. During the course of "A Wife of Nashville," the four maids practice this kind of reportage over and over. Jess, the most satisfactory of the four, sits in the back seat of the family automobile listening to John R. give John R., Jr., a driving lesson. Suddenly she volunteers that John R., Jr., is "letting the clutch out too fast." She is silent again until the boy stalls the car's engine. At that point, Jess repeats what her brother-in-law has said about handling a flooded engine, giving John R., Jr., better driving instructions than his father has. After that instance, Jess teaches all the boys how to drive, although she herself has never learned. The best she can do is parrot what she has heard.

When an earlier maid, Jane Blakemore, suggests that Helen Ruth take John R.'s Ford coupe and drive out to Thornton, Helen Ruth parrots the "answer . . . she [knows] John R. would have given." She refuses, though she feels very much the opposite. When John R. comes home on the weekends and notices how spotless their apartment is, he tells Helen Ruth she drives herself "too hard." But it is Jane Blakemore who does the work. She is the one who is driven, though only around the house, not out to Thornton.

Helen Ruth's second maid, Carrie, gossips about her employer, and Helen Ruth's statement about the disagreement she has had with her husband gets out around Nashville until she hears herself quoted: "Because a woman's husband hunts is no reason for her to hunt, any more than because a man's wife sews is any reason for him to sew." The isolation Helen Ruth feels upon hearing something so private made public is part of the increasing experience she has with vacancy. Carrie parrots what she has heard. Like an echo, she demonstrates the gap between the very different private and public instances of the same statement.

In the story reportage dramatizes the gap that exists between people. Sarah, Helen Ruth's third maid, watches as Helen Ruth threatens to call a "bluecoat" and drive off Morse, Sarah's drunken and abusive husband. Then four months later, Sarah calls, gets John R., Jr., on the telephone, and asks him to tell his mother that she is marrying "a man named Racecar and they [are] leaving for Chicago in the morning." Previously, Morse "had returned from up North" and when Helen Ruth drove him away, he ostensibly moved north again. Once Jess's departure is explained, the reader thinks back and is not certain that Sarah didn't lie (the way Jess will later) and that in fact Racecar was Morse returning once more for Sarah. The information about Sarah's departure is followed immediately with the news that, "during the Depression," Rufus Brantley, the man who had helped John R. get into the insurance business, "had shot himself through the head while cleaning a gun at his hunting lodge." The same sentence goes on to say that "most of John R.'s other hunting friends had suffered the same financial reverses that John R. had." The strong implication is that Rufus Brantley committed suicide, but the report given was that he had an accident "cleaning a gun." It seems clear that there is a gap between what happened and what Nashville society will accept—just as there is a gap created by the lie Jess tells.

Of the other instances suggesting the vacancy that lurks behind appearances, the clearest example, the one the entire story builds toward, is the lie Jess uses. She believes she must use it to extricate herself from Helen Ruth's family, in which her role has diminished as the boys have grown older. Jess arranges for a phone call to come during breakfast. Her friend Mary, with whom she is going to move to California, calls, and Jess pretends the call is a message telling her that her "little brother . . . baby brother" is dead. Jess has no such brother, and Helen Ruth has already learned through a friend about Jess's plans to leave. The same gossip that hurt Helen Ruth when Carrie worked for the family informs her now. This time Helen Ruth knows the truth, but she has not always been so alert. Not until her fourth maid is leaving her does she fully understand what is happening. By this time, Helen Ruth has more than learned what the problem is. That is why in her coda at the end of the story she keeps mentioning "lonesomeness" and "loneliness," terms that describe the way vacancy feels. Helen Ruth is reporting from a foreign land that exists within herself.

Displacement and loneliness are present from the story's beginning in the guise of Helen Ruth's double name. Helen Ruth's is a hyphenated existence. The hyphen's power to simultaneously join and separate opens a gap in which similarities and differences become apparent. The Greek Helen is yoked with the Old Testament Ruth. Both women were forced to live in foreign lands, as we discover that Nashville is foreign to Helen Ruth, and as the world of their white employers is foreign to Helen Ruth's four maids. Helen Ruth's predicament is that her husband has moved her from her hometown of Thornton to Nashville, where she is uncomfortable with his hunting set and where he leaves her alone a great deal of the time.

Helen Ruth is likened to Helen, who was abducted as a child, then again as a woman, then returned. And, on the other side of the hyphen, Helen Ruth is likened to Ruth, who accompanied her mother-in-law, Naomi, out of Ruth's homeland to Bethlehem-Judah. There, through Naomi's help, Ruth is joined with Boaz. The terms Boaz makes for Ruth are a match for Helen Ruth's husband, John R., at his most ingenious as an insurance agent. Helen Ruth's despair is figured by her being simultaneously joined and separated. She is "of" and not "of" Nashville, just as she is paired with her maids and known by her double name. These facts combine to echo the stories of Helen and Ruth, two other displaced women. The words "lonesomeness" and "loneliness," repeated so often at the story's conclusion, serve as a refrain in the coda Helen Ruth gives as she lists again the key moments that have characterized her life as the wife of a Nashville insurance executive. No one has been less insured or assured than Helen Ruth, and she recognizes this in large part through the even greater vulnerabilities faced by the four black women who have worked for her over the years, each for a longer and more satisfactory period than the one before. The triumph that Helen Ruth achieves at the story's conclusion appears out of the vacuum of her isolation and powerlessness. In contrast, her husband and sons enjoy what they consider to be the benefits of Nashville society and cannot imagine why Jess McGehee would deceive them.

Trying to explain why Jess pretended she had a "little brother" who had died in Brownsville, Tennessee, and that she was only going there for the funeral when in fact she was leaving the family for good, Helen Ruth says to her husband and three sons, "My dears, don't you see how it was for Jess? How else can they tell us anything when there is such a gulf?"

The word *gulf* performs multiple tasks. It appeals to a realization on Helen Ruth's part that is central to the story, her acceptance of isolation. Such a term also evokes racial attitudes that would have been common in the 1930s. Jess's behavior is understood by John R. and his sons through an appeal to reductional attitudes about the alleged inferiority of blacks as thinking itself is depicted as a kind of vacancy.

On another level, the "gulf" Helen Ruth identifies is not only a matter of race, gender, and economics but, most painfully, it reveals the gap on a personal level between Jess and the white people for whom she cares, ironically the same white world of family and movies from which she creates the projections that give her comfort. That is the material she pores over in her room when she is alone. Her imaginings enable her to possess, however briefly, parts of a world that nevertheless holds her off. Her white family provides compensation for her in her scrapbook the same way the Hollywood stars do in the movie magazines she exchanges with Mary. That is a preliminary approach to Jess's side of the "gulf." Helen Ruth occupies shoreline along the same opening.

If we think of "gulf" in several senses at once, the way Helen Ruth thinks of the long list of details that form an aggregate for her as an answer to Jess's way of leaving, and if we recall Helen Ruth's own worry about how to bridge the gap between herself and those supposedly closest to her, then we get another sense of the "gulf" Taylor is describing. Taylor poses Helen Ruth's problem this way:

> What could she say to them, she kept asking herself. And each time she asked the question, she received for answer some different memory of seemingly unrelated things out of the past twenty years of her life. These things presented themselves as answers to her question, and each of them seemed

satisfactory to her. But how little sense it would make to her husband and her grown sons, she reflected, if she should suddenly begin telling them about the long hours she had spent waiting in that apartment at the Vaux Hall while John R. was on the road for the Standard Candy Company, and in the same breath should tell them about how plainly she used to talk to Jane Blakemore and how Jane pretended that the baby made her nervous and went back to Thornton. Or suppose she should abruptly remind John R. of how ill at ease the wives of his hunting friends used to make her feel and how she had later driven Sarah's worthless husband out of the yard, threatening to call a bluecoat. What if she should suddenly say that because a woman's husband hunts, there is no reason for her to hunt, any more than because a man's wife sews, there is reason for him to sew.

The litany goes on, establishing the story's vision of "lonesomeness" and "loneliness." Helen Ruth has been isolated by her role as a wife, just as in a more obvious way her servants have been isolated as maids. Her husband and sons are isolated also but cannot see that. The "gulf" they border is made invisible by the pieties they invoke to make the loss of Jess normative and acceptable. All the while, Helen Ruth knows more than their comforting words can circumscribe, and part of what she knows about her despair is that she accepts it. Here "gulf" works in a more positive way. Acceptance of its existence is the first step one takes out of despair. A gulf is both an abyss and a protected water.

The "gulf" that Jess and Helen Ruth border is a kind of fold, where the two live as doubles mirroring each other yet partly out of sight and misunderstood as they at once nurture the members of their family and are forced to live at a distance from those they nurture. Helen Ruth's progress through the story is her growing awareness of the kind of vacancy that her role as a wife entails, one that is required by all those around her. Over the course of the story, she moves from a series of projections applied to her servants, which reveal what she herself in fact lacks, to an acceptance of the way things are and, more accurately, the ways things are not.

At the end of the story, Helen Ruth recalls the "'so much else' that had been missing from her life and that she had not been able to name." And she recalls "the foolish mysteries she had so nobly accepted upon her reconciliation with John R." The term *foolish mysteries* is one attempt by Helen Ruth to give a name to the tear, "gulf," or gap along which she has had to live her life. They are "foolish" because they do not explain matters. They are "mysteries" because they are thought of as somehow normative, while each individual's life is unique. The norms, the mores of a society, are part of a system of unacknowledged modifications of power. Speaking of his parents' generation during a classroom visit in 1983, Peter Taylor observed that the men exploited the women, and the women exploited the blacks. This holds true in "A Wife of Nashville," though Helen Ruth must be understood first in terms of her name and in terms of what her story's title indicates, the "of" or hyphenated existence built over a sense of vacancy faced on a daily basis.

Pairing things in ways that reveal the vacancies about which characters live is a common device in Peter Taylor's stories. In "Dean of Men" an action taken by the narrator is seen to equal something done by his father and before that, his grandfather. In "Venus, Cupid, Folly and Time" the brother and sister are paired with each other, and their arrested development matches the children they entertain. In "A Wife of Nashville" Helen Ruth is paired with her four maids, especially with the last one, Jess McGehee. The list goes on.

As a figure for despair, to what does vacancy stand opposed? That is its significance. Instead of giving assurances of her theological convictions, O'Connor does the opposite. Instead of describing an orderly Nashville society, Taylor does the opposite. In this sense, vacancy is a figure for irony by which we imagine what is in the narrative not as it is written but as it is read. By her acceptance, O'Connor's grandmother doubts doubt, while Taylor's Helen Ruth stands before her family, gives her coda, and negates negation. Kierkegaard identifies the unfortunate fact that "no sooner has one discussed something than he is the thing himself." O'Connor and Taylor understand this. There are things they do not discuss but leave to the figure of vacancy.

Contributors

RUSSELL BANKS is the author of fourteen books of fiction, most recently the novels *Affliction, The Sweet Hereafter,* and *Cloudsplitter* and the collection of new and selected short stories *The Angel on the Roof.* He lives in upstate New York and in Princeton, New Jersey.

JOHN CASEY won the National Book Award in 1989. He won the Mildred and Harold Strauss Living Award from the American Academy of Arts and Letters for the period 1992 to 1997. His latest novel is *The Half-Life of Happiness.* Professor of English at the University of Virginia, he resides in Charlottesville.

ELLEN DOUGLAS, who has taught at the Sewanee Writers' Conference for six years, lives in Jackson, Mississippi. The author of six previous volumes, her latest book is *Truth: Four Stories I'm Finally Old Enough to Tell.*

HORTON FOOTE has received Academy Awards for his screenplays *To Kill a Mockingbird* and *Tender Mercies,* and his play *The Man from Atlanta* was awarded the Pulitzer Prize in 1995. He is a member of the Southern Writers of the American Academy of Arts and Letters, from which he received the Gold Medal for Drama for the entire body of his work. His memoir, *Farewell*, was published in 1999.

ERNEST J. GAINES is the author of six novels, the story collection *Bloodline*, and a children's book. His latest novel, *A Lesson before Dying*, won the National Book Critics Circle Award and was chosen by Oprah Winfrey as a Book of the Month. He is Writer in Residence at the University of Louisiana at Lafayette.

ANTHONY HECHT is the author of seven books of poems and three books of essays and criticism. He is a member of the American Academy of Arts and Letters and is a recipient of numerous honors, including the Pulitzer Prize, the Bollingen Prize, and the Aiken Taylor, Ruth B. Lilly, and Frost awards.

JOHN HOLLANDER's *Reflections on Espionage*, with a new introduction and notes, has just been reissued; his previous book of poetry was *Figurehead and Other Poems*. He is Sterling Professor of English at Yale University and recently gave the Clark Lectures at Cambridge.

DIANE JOHNSON is a novelist and critic who divides her time between Paris and San Francisco. Her recent publications include *Le Divorce* and *Le Mariage*, two novels set in France. She is a member of the American Academy of Arts and Letters.

DONALD JUSTICE's most recent collection of poems is *New and Selected Poems* (1998), and his most recent collection of criticism is *Oblivion* (1995). In 1980 he received the Pulitzer Prize for poetry and in 1991, the Bollingen Prize.

ROMULUS LINNEY is the author of three novels and many plays, produced throughout the United States and abroad. He recently received the Award of Merit Medal from the American Academy of Arts and Letters.

ALICE McDERMOTT is the author of four novels, the latest of which is *Charming Billy*, for which she received the National Book Award. She is Writer in Residence at Johns Hopkins University.

MARSHA NORMAN is the author of the Pulitzer Prize–winning play *'Night, Mother* and, more recently, of *Trudy Blue*. Her Broadway musical *The Secret Garden* received both Tony and Drama Desk awards. She lives in New York, where she is cochair of the Playwriting Department of the Juilliard School.

FRANCINE PROSE is the author of ten novels, most recently *Blue Angel*. *Guided Tours of Hell*, a collection of novellas, appeared in 1997. She is currently a fellow of the New York Institute for the Humanities and of the New York Public Library's Center for Scholars and Writers.

WYATT PRUNTY has recently published his sixth collection of poems, *Unarmed and Dangerous: New and Selected Poems*. He is the author of *Fallen from the Symboled World: Precedents for the New Formalism*, a discussion of contemporary poetry. He teaches English at the University of the South at Sewanee, where he founded and directs the Sewanee Writers' Conference and edits the Sewanee Writers' Series.

Index